THE FUNDAMENTALS OF
PUTTING

FRANK THOMAS
& VALERIE MELVIN

FRANKLY

FRANKLY

A FRANKLY PUBLICATION
Reunion Resort and Club
7599 Gathering Drive
Reunion, Florida 34747
www.franklygolf.com

Published throughout the world by Frankly Golf.

ISBN-10: 0615726917
ISBN-13: 978-0-615-72691-5

Designed by Tim Oliver
Illustrations by Grant Carruthers
Edited by Steve Donahue

First edition.
Second printing.

DEDICATION

I would like to dedicate this book to my father, who introduced me to golf. He was an avid student of the game and follower of Ben Hogan's Fundamentals. He taught me that golf was a gentleman's game and I should behave accordingly, and respect the game and my fellow competitors. He taught me to remove my hat whenever I shook hands, be it at the beginning or end of a round, and never to wear my hat in the clubhouse. Old-fashioned ideas, maybe, but we are playing an old-fashioned game.

— FRANK THOMAS

HOW TO BENEFIT MOST FROM THIS BOOK

MOST OF THIS BOOK'S PREPARATION was related to shortening it as much as possible without compromising the content or readability. We have consequently supplemented the text with many illustrations.

We ask you to apply the fundamentals in the order they are presented because The Fundamentals of Putting is a Stroke and Mind-set building process, with each of the Fundamentals being a prerequisite to the subsequent one.

We need a properly fitted putter that provides a solid foundation upon which we will be able to BUILD a sound stroke. If the foundation is defective, every building block thereafter carries with it a compensating factor to cope with something that does not fit properly and only fractures the stroke's integrity, adding to an inconsistent result.

We should recognize that once we have learned, applied and practiced the Fundamentals to develop our ability, putting becomes a matter of subconsciously letting this happen, just like throwing a dart or a ball. We then need to learn how to control the mind not to interfere with this natural ability.

Once we learn and practice the fundamentals we must allow them to become subconscious actions and then rely on our natural ability to make the putt.

Read, Understand, Learn, Practice and then — "Let it Happen."

Please enjoy,
Frank & Valerie

CONTENTS

BACKGROUND

THE FOUNDERS OF Frankly, Frank Thomas and Valerie Melvin are uniquely qualified to present "The Fundamentals of Putting" to golfers interested in improving their putting and enjoyment of the game, and to instructors interested in making their instruction more effective by providing structured, systematic and technically sound lessons to their students.

Prior to Frank Thomas redirecting his extensive golf knowledge and talents toward putting research and instruction, he invented the Graphite Shaft in 1969 as chief design engineer for Shakespeare Sporting Goods Co. In 1974, Frank joined the United States Golf Association as Technical Director, where he was responsible for the development of the golf industry's most-advanced Research and Test Center and assembled a research-and-test team unsurpassed in golf.

In 1977, Frank redesigned and introduced the "Stimpmeter" to golf. The Stimpmeter is now used worldwide to measure the speed of greens.

In 1979, Frank assembled and directed the Handicap Research Team, which modified and refined the handicap system. He, with the support of research team members, introduced and directed the GHIN handicap system.

After 26 years with the USGA Frank co-founded Frankly Consulting and Frankly Golf to help golfers, and conduct research on putting and putting instruction. As the Chief Technical Advisor to both *Golf Digest* and The Golf Channel he helped golfers better understand golf's technical side through articles and TV appearances.

Frank's knowledge of The Fundamentals of Putting is unsurpassed in golf and, with Valerie Melvin and her knowledge of the psychology and mental side of putting, they have introduced the most-advanced understanding of the putting stroke and revolutionized putting instruction.

Valerie Melvin joined Frank after serving as editor of Golf Science International (GSI), a magazine published by the World Scientific Congress of Golf. Prior to GSI Valerie represented Scotland in international competition. The time spent on the putting green was central to her development as an international amateur golfer, and made her uniquely qualified to understand and teach putting.

Valerie studied psychology at Stirling University and conducted research on brain activity prior to the golf putt. She completed her Masters degree in medical science with a focus on Sport and Exercise.

Over the last 12 years, Valerie and Frank have devoted their time to researching and teaching the mechanics of the putting stroke and applying an understanding of what is happening in the mind when putting. They have taught many young golfers such as Andy Zhang — the youngest golfer (14) to have ever qualified for the U.S. Open (2012) — and spent time working with Tour players.

The holistic approach they developed attracted the PGA of Great Britain and Ireland to partner with Frankly Academies and develop an online Certified Putting Instructor (CPI) curriculum for PGA professionals.

The Frankly Academies' CPI course is supported by an Advisory Board, of which 10 members have PhDs in various golf-related disciplines and are respected researchers in golf.

Teaching people how to putt has now become a structured and systematic science, rather than a disorderly art form.

Seven PGAs around the world, including the LPGA and college coaches (GCAA), have adopted the CPI online putting course to help their members further their education, improve their ability to teach putting and enhance their status as professionals.

An online course covering The Fundamentals of Putting is now available to golfers. Those interested in further improving and maintaining their putting skill are urged to review this online course, which is enhanced with 40 videos and more detail of everything in this book.

NOTE:
Even the best putters need an occasional tune-up, so if you're serious about your game, we recommend you contact a CPI or visit the Putting PAD (Performance Analysis & Development) at Reunion Resort in Orlando, Florida. *www.FranklyGolf.com*

SPECIAL NOTE:
While this book is based on scientific principles, we have tried to keep the scientific nomenclature to a minimum to more effectively get the message across to our friends, especially those of you who are not scientifically inclined.

For those who are inclined to delve into the nitty-gritty of the science, we have referenced some excellent papers and literature, much of which has influenced our teachings. These references can be found in the Appendix, but of specific interest are proceedings of the World Scientific Congress of Golf meetings.

INTRODUCTION

WHEN WE COME TO TERMS with the fact that between 40 percent to 45 percent of our score are putts and we spend about the same percentage of time on the putting green, we recognize the importance of putting.

Putting is a skill we have ignored because it is not promoted by golf instructors nor is it as sexy as driving the ball a long way. Instructors do not provide comprehensive putting lessons to their students because putting instruction is not clearly understood.

Putting instruction has been handed down, for the most part, informally from father to son. This is no different for the PGA professionals who learned from their fathers or magazines, but few have taught based on a formal putting instruction education because, until now, there has been none available.

When I asked Jack Nicklaus who taught him how to putt, he said:

"My father, who introduced me to all sports as I grew up, is the one who introduced me to the game of golf when I was 10 years old, so it was my father who gave me my first basics in putting. Once he turned me over to my long-time instructor, Jack Grout, I am sure it was Jack who gave me the fundamentals I then needed.

"Looking at my style, there wasn't really anybody who played that way," Nicklaus added. "I believe Jack Grout gave me the fundamentals of what he wanted me to do — my eyes over the line and not out over the ball — but we never talked about a stroke. My putting style was largely my own."

Imagine how much better Jack might have been if he had access to today's equipment and scientifically based instruction such as "The Fundamentals of Putting" when he was 10 years old.

Many instructors are ill-equipped and without the appropriate tools to provide systematic, structured and scientifically sound putting instruction to their students. Instead, they rely on a cursory method that works for them but does not do this aspect of the game any justice.

When we were very young, we had no fear, which allowed us to putt well with complete and unwavering confidence. We didn't question or even try to understand how or why we did so well, we just did it. When things are going well, why question it?

In many cases, because we never had any formal training nor understood how we acquired our natural ability to putt well — a few tips from a relative, what we saw others doing and our unbridled enthusiasm were the only ingredients — when these abilities faltered, and we started to "lose the magic," we had nowhere to turn to recover. This is a common affliction of many maturing golfers, including the very elite.

In fact, what we have lost is the ability to let our natural talent exhibit itself. Because we occasionally lose our focus and falter, we start losing trust in our own abilities, and we contrive and manipulate our stroke based on a quick-fix suggestion from someone who has never seen our stroke. As a last resort and, out of pure desperation to recapture that lost magic, we consider buying a new putter.

Recreating the magic by understanding why and how we putted so well during our youth is what this book will do for us, whether we just want to improve our putting, are desperate or otherwise. The book will provide a clear understanding of The Fundamentals of Putting based on sound scientific principles, in a comprehensive but simple, systematic and structured manner, allowing the reader to help himself/herself.

The principles are simple, clear and, if applied, will allow the body, through repetition, to subconsciously move the way it wants to move, not in the way the conscious mind — sometimes cluttered with all sorts of strange ideas acquired after losing the magic — tries to direct the body to move.

After the conscious mind understands the fundamentals and instructs the body how to apply them, it must relinquish control, get out of its own way, let the body and subconscious mind take over, and then

Let it Happen.

PART I:
THE FUNDAMENTALS OF PUTTING
& THE SIX DEGREES OF FREEDOM

Putting Well

PUTTING WELL is the act of being able to replicate an acquired ability, i.e. the putting stroke, without having to think about it. The body must perform as trained by the mind, which in turn must have confidence and believe in a successful outcome.

First, we must understand what we need to do, and it certainly helps to know why — i.e. the fundamentals of how to position the body and make the movements.

Second, we need to practice the fundamentals repeatedly, allowing the mind to gradually relinquish instructional control of the body, and "get out of its own way."*

Third, having trained the body to perform the act proficiently we must let it respond to the subconscious.

And then, Let it Happen.

Six Degrees of Freedom (DoF)

WE WILL NOW COVER and explain the six Degrees of Freedom (DoF) in putting, which you will not find anywhere else in putting instruction. Understanding the six DoF is one of the secrets of making a good stroke and knowing why.

A DoF is the freedom of movement about a specific axis. Because this movement cannot be performed exactly the same way each time, there is a range within which this movement is made. This range is the source of error of that DoF,

Instinct Putting (see page 172 for reference)

and each DoF carries with it a source of error.

For example, one of the six DOF is the breaking of the wrists during the putting stroke. It is difficult to make or time this break consistently. As a result, the wrists will break a little differently — more or less — from one putt to another for similar length putts. The variation of wrist-break amount and wrist-break tempo is the tolerance — plus or minus — we must accept. Lowering this tolerance (error) would be ideal, but this takes time.

In other words, the wrist break is a source of error. If you minimize — constrain — this wrist-break or eliminate it you minimize or eliminate the source of error and will increase your consistency.

Throughout this book we will refer to and explain how to restrain or eliminate the DoF, thus minimizing or eliminating the source of error associated with each.

The true secret of becoming a good putter is the ability to understand why and how you make a good stroke and how to minimize the errors.

The six DOF in putting are:

1) **UP AND DOWN** — moving the putter up and down off the putting surface.
2) **IN AND OUT** — moving the putter toward or away from the body.
3) **BACK AND FORTH** — this movement is essential if we want to transfer momentum from the putter head to the ball, i.e. hit the ball.
4) **WRIST BREAK** — this movement involves bending the wrists. We refer to the person doing this as a "wristy" putter.
5) **WRIST ROTATION** — this is a forearm and wrist rotation opening and closing the face of the putter.
6) **WEIGHT SHIFT** — this movement shifts weight or sways during the stroke.

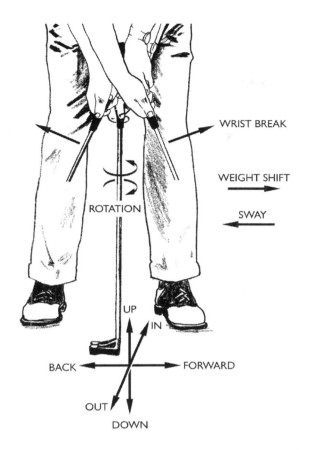

SUMMARY

Knowing and understanding the six DoF — and applying the fundamentals — will minimize their effect and the sources of error associated with each, leading to greater putting consistency.

DOF ARE: 1. Up and down 2. In and out 3. Back and forth 4. Wrist break 5. Wrist and forearm rotation 6. Sway (weight shift)

Let's Begin to Let it Happen

ONE OF THE MOST important ingredients in becoming a great putter is to learn where and how we generate sources of error. An understanding of the basic movements of the body and the putting stroke will allow us to adjust, limit and/or refine these to eliminate sources of error. Being aware of the various movements — DoF — is the first step. There is nothing mysterious about the DoF, and understanding them is very simple.

DIAGNOSE
YOUR
PUTTING
SKILLS

ITH VERY *few exceptions, we can all putt better, no matter who we are, or how long we have been playing golf.* ¶ In this short chapter, we need to define the areas of weakness in our putting as we perceive them, then focus on these as we proceed through the fundamentals and building our stroke. ¶ Golf has evolved very slowly over 500 years and this lends some degree of constancy, and in turn a degree of stability, to our lives as golfers. Along with this almost stagnant evolution in the game there is a pervasive acquiescence that what my father taught me – and his father taught him – is all I need to know.

As we previously discussed, this hand-me-down process is especially true when it comes to putting and how many of us learned to putt. PGA professionals are no different. We should be concerned that most teaching professionals have not been formally trained to provide comprehensive putting instruction. This is why there are so many varied methods and techniques in the minimal amount of dedicated putting instruction provided.

Before we start working to correct our weaknesses let's define what they are or perceived to be:

There are probably several areas of perceived weak spots in our putting, so place a check mark beside those areas below where you think your putting could be improved. This will help us focus more attention on those fundamentals that address these issues as we proceed through the book.

COMMON AREAS OF WEAKNESS ARE:

- Distance control _____
- Alignment and accuracy _____
- Short putts _____
- Long putts _____
- Reading greens _____
- Focus _____
- Confidence _____
- Inconsistency _____
- Yips _____
- Confidence in your putter _____
- Other _____

Once we have checked the areas of our putting that we think need help, then we need to be honest with ourselves and evaluate our putting skills on a (1 - 10) basis, with (10) being perfect and (1) being "need a lot of help."

How do you rate your putting skills **NOW** ? _____

Return to this page after reading the book and rerate your putting skills **AFTER** _____

This self-rating process will certainly change once you have applied the teachings in this book, and will provide you with confidence and the belief that you CAN sink every putt.

SUMMARY

Identify and define your weaknesses and rate your putting skills, then work to strengthen these and work diligently on those areas that need the most help. Once you have read the book and applied the teachings, you need to return to this page and again rate your putting skills, which will help build your confidence.

2

HOW
TO FIT
YOUR
PUTTER

I T WOULD CERTAINLY BE irresponsible to teach you how to drive a car before adjusting the seats so you can reach the pedals and see what's behind you in the rear-view and side-view mirrors. ¶ It is equally irresponsible to start a program to improve and build your putting stroke before you are correctly fitted for a putter. This chapter relates to standard (conventional) putters, but we will cover Long, Belly and Side-Saddle putters later in the book in Chapter 14.

Step No. 1

S EVERAL STEPS to follow in fitting a putter require that you position yourself over the ball correctly in a comfortable and balanced putting posture (*see sketch alongside*).

The knees are slightly bent with weight evenly distributed on both feet, and between the balls and heels of each foot.

The feet should be about 12 to 18 inches apart at the toes.

The upper torso is bent forward with the lower back tilted forward at about 45 degrees and the neck is almost horizontal.

This is the most common PUTTING POSTURE, which has evolved over about 500 years and relatively easy to replicate and reasonably comfortable.

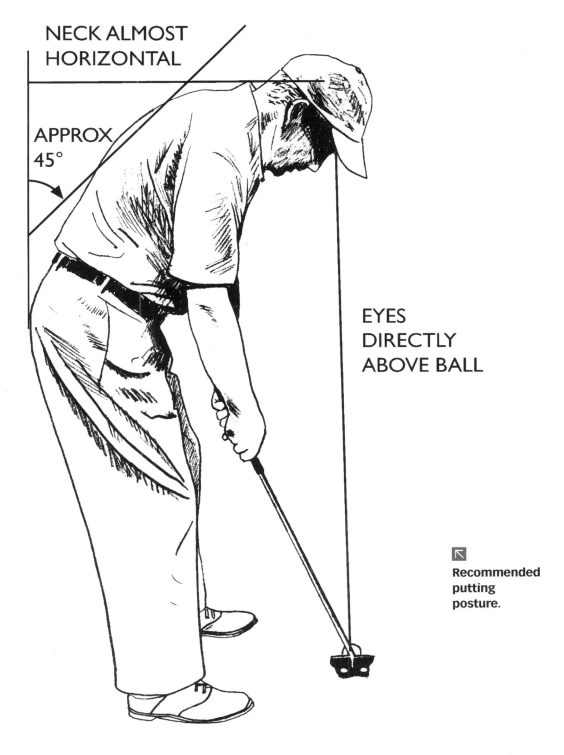

NECK ALMOST
HORIZONTAL

APPROX
45°

EYES
DIRECTLY
ABOVE BALL

Recommended
putting
posture.

Step No. 2

THE BALL SHOULD BE directly below the eyes. To find this correct ball position, place a mirror on the green or on the floor. Place a coin (which represents the ball) on the mirror and then take a normal putting posture with your head over the mirror.

Now move your body until you see the reflection of your eyes in the mirror right above the coin. Move your feet closer to, or away from, the mirror. DO NOT LEAN forward or back. Measure the distance from your toes to the coin, which will be approximately six to eight inches, or about two putter heads. Try to remember this for future reference.

If you don't have a mirror, you can use a piece of string attached to your key chain and hang this from the bridge of your nose. The ball (coin) should be directly below the key chain.

It will help if you have established the distance from the ball (coin) to your feet, when your eyes are over the ball in your comfortable putting posture, because we will need to get into this position while building our putting stroke.

Step No. 3

NOW THAT YOU KNOW the ball should be six to eight inches from your feet, which in turn are about 12 to 18 inches apart, position the putter face at this distance centered between your feet.

Place the putter head behind the ball and allow your hands to slide down or up the grip portion of the putter as your arms straighten, letting them hang from your shoulders. When doing this DO NOT change your putting posture.

With your arms in this relaxed hanging mode, take your normal grip on the putter. Try not to grip the putter at the end of the putter's grip — simply because that is where the end of the grip is — but take your grip with your arms rela-

ARMS RELAXED AND STRAIGHT, BUT NOT STIFF

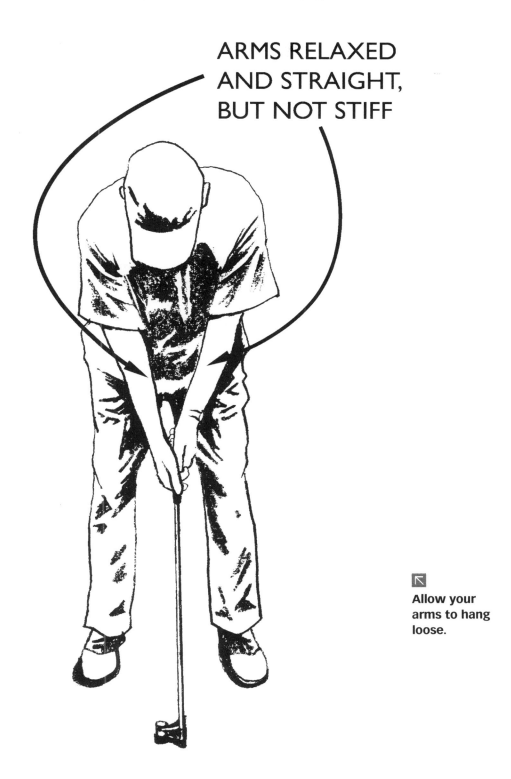

Allow your arms to hang loose.

tively straight. The position of your hands may be partially on the shaft of the putter.

Now you need to measure the distance from the heel of the upper hand to the end of the putter grip. Subtract this from the length of the putter and add a half-inch. This is the correct length for your putter.

EXAMPLE: Your putter is 35 inches long. The distance from the heel of your upper hand to the end of the putter grip is three inches. Subtracting three from 35 equals 32 inches. Adding a half-inch to 32 equals 32½ inches. The correct length of your putter should be 32½ inches from the butt end of the grip to the sole of the putter.

NOTE: The length of the putter may vary depending on your preferred gripping style (we will cover gripping styles in the next chapter). Before you shorten your putter place a piece of tape on the grip at a point a half-inch above the heel portion of the upper hand.

If you find that you are bending over too much and with your arms relatively straight, the putter may be too short, which is very unusual but possible.

You will now be able to proceed working on the fundamentals gripping the putter below the tape marking the proper putter length, which can be shortened later.

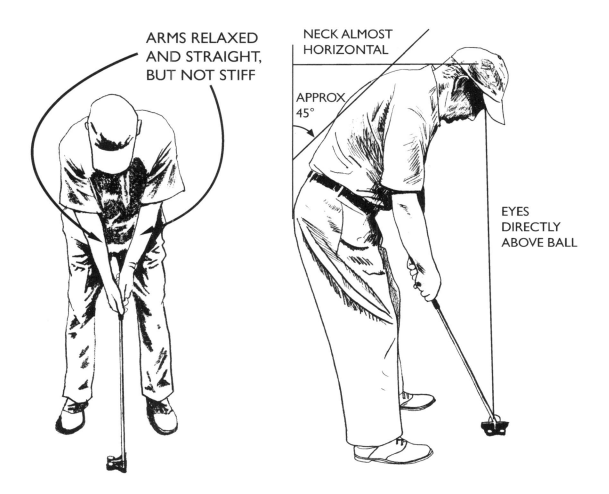

ARMS RELAXED
AND STRAIGHT,
BUT NOT STIFF

NECK ALMOST
HORIZONTAL

APPROX
45°

EYES
DIRECTLY
ABOVE BALL

SUMMARY

Fit the putter such that your posture is comfortable, well balanced and the ball is directly below the eyes. Then make sure your arms are relaxed and relatively straight. In most cases putters are too long for golfers and don't allow them to make a natural swing because of too much tension in the arms which, in most cases, are bent to accommodate the putter which is too long.

3

THE
GRIP

ELECTING A WELL-DESIGNED, properly fitted putter is important (we will cover putter design in Chapter 15). However, once this putter selection has been made and properly fitted, we need to learn how to use it. ¶ We advise our students that buying a good instrument alone will not make us into better putters, no matter what advertising claims are made or how much we believe in magic. There is no sense in buying a Ferrari and then driving it like a tractor.

NOTE: To avoid confusion in this chapter we will refer to the grip of the putter as "The Grip" and the way you hold this as "Our or Your Grip." As we proceed through the chapter and the rest of the book the context in which we use the word "grip" should be clear as to whether it is the way you hold the putter or the putter grip itself.

Almost as important as having a correctly fitted putter is the way we hold it — i.e. our grip.

REVERSE OVERLAP GRIP

THERE ARE NUMEROUS WAYS to hold a putter. The first way we suggest is to hold the putter in the same manner most commonly used by many of the world's best golfers — "The Reverse Overlap grip." This does not mean that everybody should use this grip, but it is the style we recommend for most golfers. There are various other methods to hold a putter, which we will cover later.

The Reverse Overlap requires that you first grip the putter with the right hand, if you are right-handed, at the lower portion of the grip of the putter — if your putter is of the correct length. Place the right thumb on top but close to the bottom portion of the grip. This should be a natural, comfortable grip — do not try to manipulate this to be in the fingers or along the lifeline, etc. Just grip it comfortably.

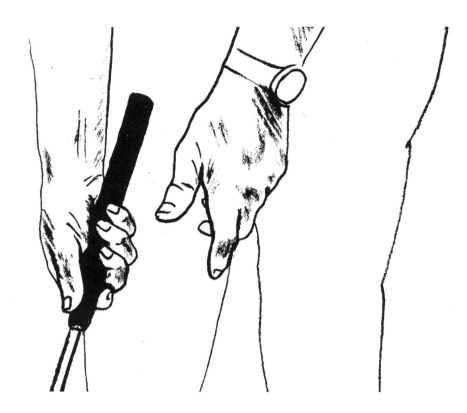

Then move the left hand over the right with the left thumb snuggled under the meaty portion of the right thumb, and touching the tips of the right hand's ring and pinky fingers. The left hand's index finger should then rest over the right hand's pinky and ring finger (*see illustration above*).

Slight variations of this grip might be a little more comfortable, but as close to this as possible is good.

With this Reverse Overlap grip both thumbs are on the flat side (top) of the putter grip — generally putter grips have a flat topside.

It is strongly suggested that we do not extend the right index finger straight down the shaft or the left index finger straight down over the right fingers as this adds unnecessary

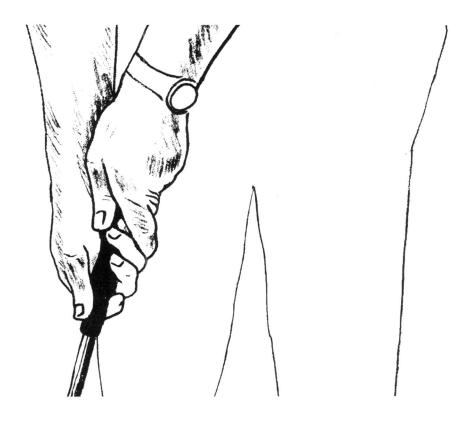

tension in the forearms, which is something we must try to avoid.

This gripping method is called the "Reverse Overlap" as opposed to the regular overlap, or "Vardon" grip," commonly used for the full-swing clubs where the right pinky overlaps the left index finger. The "Interlocking grip" for the full swing — i.e. left index finger interlocking with the right pinky — is used by the likes of Jack Nicklaus, Tiger Woods and Valerie Melvin.

We make a distinction between the full-swing grip — either the Vardon grip or the Interlocking grip — and the reverse overlap, because the tighter gripping pressure required to hold the full-swing club prevents the club from slipping

First place your right hand on the grip (*left*), then add your left hand as shown at right.

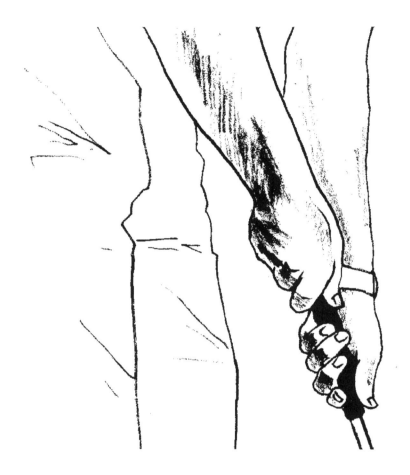

out of our hands. A significantly lighter grip pressure is required when holding the putter.

Applying excess grip pressure to a putter during the putting stroke only adds tension and contributes to inconsistent
results affecting good rhythm — sometimes referred to as
"good tempo" — and distance control.

We must get rid of all forms of tension in the arms, wrists
and hands if we are to have good rhythm (we will cover
rhythm in Chapter Eight).

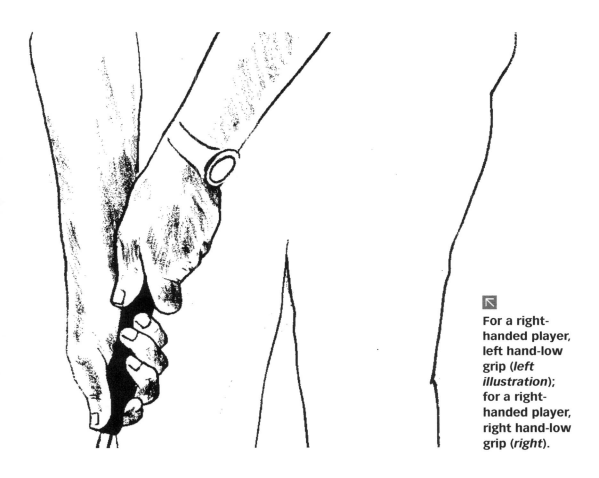

For a right-handed player, left hand-low grip (*left illustration*); for a right-handed player, right hand-low grip (*right*).

OTHER GRIP OPTIONS

Split Grip

OTHER GRIPS TO CONSIDER that may be very effective for a number of golfers are the split grip with either hand — left or right — below the other without any overlap but with the hands just touching each other and the thumbs on the top flat side of the grip.

One of the advantages of the split grip is that it allows the arm of the lower hand to be almost straight, creating a relaxed but almost straight continuous structure of arm/hand/ putter shaft. This connection between the shoulder, the putter head and a split grip helps minimize the wrist break, which is a DoF (Degree of Freedom) we want to restrain as much as possible but without tension.

A wrist break where the putter pivots around the wrists or features a slight whipping motion is a very common problem for golfers.

Very few elite golfers have ever been able to perfect this wrist break and, when they have, it required hours of practice every day for many years.

Unfortunately, these elite golfers didn't have access to the knowledge we have today about the putting stroke, which would have cut down significantly on the time required to perfect their stroke. It just shows you how great they were and how much dedication and perseverance they had.

A golfer trying to improve his or her putting must avoid the wrist break as it leads to inconsistencies in both distance and direction control.

The most important thing to remember is that a light, minimum-pressure grip is important and will contribute to good rhythm and a natural stroke.

Assuming you have selected to use one of the grips discussed above we can move on to the next chapter.

Experimenting with a different grip style is not a problem as long as it doesn't affect the rest of your stroke or the other fundamentals.

Dominant hand

WE NEED TO RECOGNIZE that in some cases the hands are inclined to vie for dominance rather than work in synchrony or allow one to be the leader and dominate, with the other one being passive and going along for the ride.

This fighting of the hands for dominance will cause inconsistencies in the stroke, affecting direction and distance control. Fighting hands can also affect the swing plane (which we will discuss in Chapter Seven).

Fighting hands is common and another reason for selecting a split grip. In some cases, using a Claw grip (i.e., when a right hander uses a split grip and the lower hand — right hand — is turned upside down and holds the club between the lower hand's thumb and index finger) solves this problem. This will help us — not our hands — make the decision as to which hand should dominate while the other remains passive.

Once you perfect the one-hand practice drill described in Chapter Eight (Finding Your Natural Rhythm), it is sometimes a good thought when putting to THINK that you are putting with one hand and the other is going along for the ride. This will prevent the hands from vying for dominance and help smooth out your putting stroke.

CUT YOUR PUTTER TO LENGTH

ONCE YOU HAVE SELECTED a method to grip the putter, stick with it until it becomes comfortable. You must avoid any discomfort in your posture or the way you hold the putter, as these will distract you from building your stroke and applying the other Fundamentals.

Thus, it is important that at this stage you cut (or extend) your putter to the correct length.

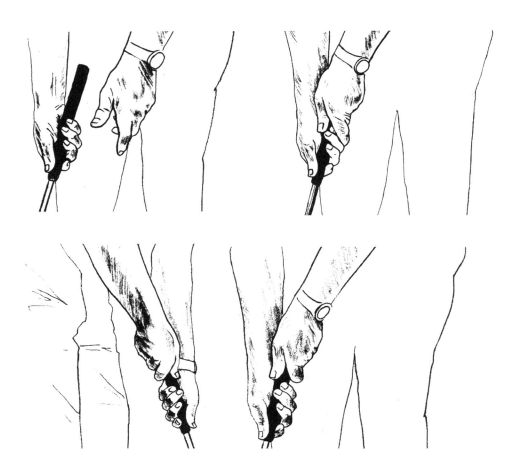

SUMMARY

Have a comfortable but light grip and don't let your hands fight each other. Select a method to hold the putter that best suits you, then cut your putter to the correct length. This will help remove doubt and allow you to focus on building your stroke. Remember that a light grip is essential for good rhythm, which in turn helps distance control.

4

BALL
POSITION
&
WHY

"ONE OF THE most important things with me when putting is to make sure my lines are proper. By that, I want to make certain my eyes are on the line of the putter. If you drop the ball from your eyes, it would be on the line of where you're putting — I would keep my eyes on that or inside it." *—Jack Nicklaus.*

With the full swing, the ball position will change depending on the club you select and the way you need to play the shot, such as the lie of the ball and your stance.

BUT when we are putting — same lie and same stance — the ball position should remain consistent relative to our body and stance. This must be the same every time we set up to the ball for every putt.

Maintaining a consistent ball position will require some practice until it becomes second nature.

Ball position is very important if we want to have consistent results, for several reasons:

• First, it will help in alignment of the putter face at address and improving direction control at impact.

• Second, it will help in presenting the same face loft and swing-path rise angle to the ball at impact, improving distance control.

• Third, if slight changes have to be made to impact conditions we will have a base line from which to work to make the corrections and recalibrate.

WHAT IS THE CORRECT BALL POSITION?

WITH YOUR TOES approximately 12 to 18 inches apart — depending on your physique and what you find most comfortable — the preferred ball position is slightly ahead of center between the feet, i.e. closer to the left foot (if right handed), by a little more than half the diameter of the ball.

This would mean that if the putter face, at address, is directly behind the ball it will be centered between the feet.

Some golfers may prefer to have the ball slightly forward or back from the recommended position because they feel more comfortable or they have a large offset putter.

However, we should know what the consequences are of moving too far off the centerline, as it will affect the putter face angle (right or left of the target) at impact, as well as the horizontal path and rise angle.

If the ball position is not consistent, it will be very difficult to make meaningful adjustments and the results will be inconsistent.

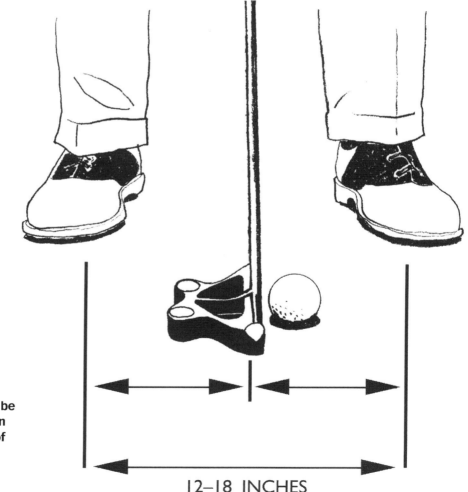

↗
The putter face should be positioned in the center of the stance.

12–18 INCHES

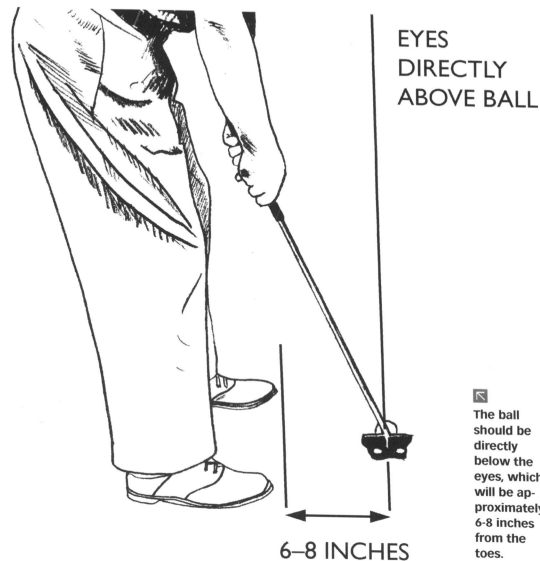

EYES
DIRECTLY
ABOVE BALL

6–8 INCHES

DISTANCE AWAY FROM THE FEET

The ball should be directly below the eyes, which will be approximately 6-8 inches from the toes.

THE RECOMMENDED POSITION of the ball is on the target line directly under our eyes when we are addressing the ball ready to make a stroke. This is an easy-to-find and consistent reference point, and the same ball position we used to fit the putter in Chapter 2 and should be used every time we set up to make a putt.

Having the ball under your eyes will help your alignment, as you are better able to see the line at which you are aiming when your eyes, the ball and the target line are all in the same vertical plane.

It is more difficult to align the putter face if your eyes are not directly over the ball/target line. To give you some idea about the difficulty, try moving about two feet away from the vertical plane — i.e. over the ball — and line up the putter face to a target point on the green. This experiment will demonstrate why it is better to be directly over the ball looking down the target line rather than too far away and from the side of the target line.

This preferred ball position with the putter face directly behind the ball will allow the putter face to present itself correctly to the ball — at right angles to the target line — at impact, and do this consistently if the swing is in-plane (we will cover Swing Plane in Chapter Seven).

Another good reason for having a consistent ball position at address is that it tends to give you a sense of comfort in knowing that you don't have to worry about it and just do it the same way each time as you prepare to make the stroke.

Being properly prepared is important and gives you confidence that — if all else is right — you have a good chance to make the putt, i.e. increasing your belief that you can sink it.

You do need to practice getting into this correct ball position until it becomes so natural that you may do it without thinking. A technique you can use to do this is to carefully position yourself in your normal PUTTING POSTURE with your eyes over the ball as described above and in the Putter Fitting section (Chapter Two).

Now insert some tees into the ground where the toes of your feet are — about 12 to 18 inches apart and parallel to the target line. Insert another tee into the ground, or place the ball or coin on the green directly below your eyes and a half-inch to one inch forward of center between your toes.

Step away from this marked setup position and back to it as many times as needed, each time taking your normal address position with your putter. Each time you get into this address position look at the target along the target line – at the hole if it is a straight putt. This will allow you to get the feeling of what it is like to set up correctly so you can do it without thinking.

If you have a slight variation of this setup position that feels a lot more comfortable to you because you have been doing it for years, and you have perfected it and are not willing to change, then use it — BUT use the tees to make sure you can do it consistently.

As mentioned before, Jack Nicklaus said that his "putting style was largely my own." This is a case where trying to make a significant change is not recommended. Jack perfected his unusual style.

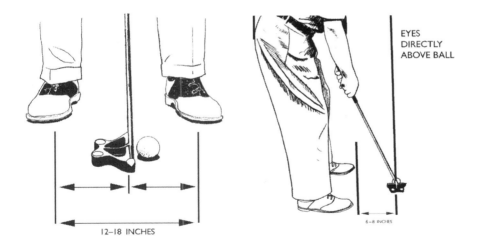

12–18 INCHES

EYES DIRECTLY ABOVE BALL

6–8 INCHES

SUMMARY
The ball position should be between the feet — toes about 12 to 18 inches apart — about half the ball diameter forward of the centerline, but directly below the eyes. The feet are lined up parallel to the target line and the putter face should be on the centerline between the feet.

ALIGNMENT
&
WHY

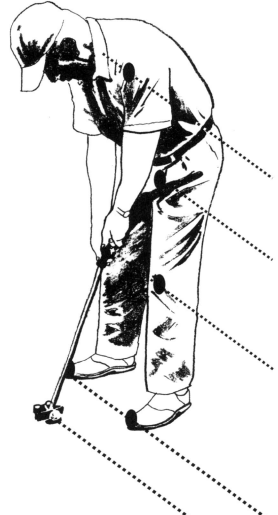

→
Ideally, all of your body lines should be parallel.

I F YOU EXPECT your putts to go in a specific direction, you must first align your body correctly. This will allow the body to make a natural symmetrical stroke that moves in a "Plane" (we will cover Swing Plane in Chapter Seven). If our feet, knees, hips and shoulders are all aligned parallel to each other we are more likely to make a stroke along the same lines – along a parallel path when the body is moving in a balanced, symmetrical path.

When the body makes a pendulum-type motion it wants to do this with the least amount of work. A pendulum best describes this movement of least resistance, a reciprocating, or alternating, motion backward and forward. Even though the swing plane is inclined at 10 degrees from the vertical, the motion in that swing plane is similar to a pendulum that is in a vertical plane.

If the body is symmetrically aligned with the target line, then the swing plane parallel to these lines is the most natural motion and generally a movement with the minimal amount of additional effort.

If the stance with the legs, feet and hips is open or closed, but the shoulders and upper body are properly aligned, then there is some conflict in the forces to move the system in preferred parallel planes.

Similarly, there should be no conflict between the preferred swing planes and the other major body segments, i.e. the feet/legs, hips and shoulders.

The whole body will behave best if aligned properly. This is the best and preferred starting point. Slight — and we emphasize SLIGHT — variations from this are acceptable, but the farther away from this you deviate the more conflict your body will have to stay in sync.

SUMMARY

Make sure that you avoid conflicting body parts by aligning all body segments, feet, hips and shoulders parallel to the ball/target-line plane.

LOCK
THE SYSTEM
&
ROCK IT

B EFORE WE MOVE ON let's take stock of what we have covered so far chapter by chapter. ¶ We have: 1) Defined and listed our weaknesses. 2) Fitted the putter. 3) Described how to hold the putter (our grip) and the importance of a light grip. 4) Determined the correct ball position to be sure that the club and ball are oriented correctly and will be in the right place and orientation at the right time. 5) Turned to Mother Nature, who likes symmetry for proper alignment of the body to make a stress-free symmetrical movement. ¶ We are now going to cover the sixth Fundamental — the "Lock the System and Rock it."

In the preface to Chapter One, we discussed the Six Degrees of Freedom (DoF) and in this chapter we start to explain how to minimize the sources of error by restraining rather than eliminating the DoF in more detail.

We call this chapter "Lock and Rock" because locking or fixing the shoulders, elbows, wrists and hand joints — as if these are a single unit or system — is exactly what we need to do. We will refer to this fixed unit as The System.

When we fitted the putter in Chapter Two we had our arms hanging vertically, or close to it. This is a natural and preferred position and used by some very good putters as you might have noticed by watching Rory McIlroy, Brandt Snedeker, Dustin Johnson, Tiger Woods and many other golfers with good mechanics.

We would like to believe that they are doing this based on a clear understanding of good and sound putting mechanics rather than an intuitive, natural, very effective acquired ability, which tends to make them consistently good putters.

Whatever the case they do it and they do it very well.

It is when they falter that they need to return to the basic mechanics and apply the fundamentals to get back on track.

In some cases the left or right arm may be slightly more bent than the other, which will reduce shoulder tilt.

If a golfer is right handed and has a Reverse Overlap grip, and the arms are relatively straight, then the left shoulder will be slightly higher than the right at address.

This slightly tilted shoulder position is not a problem. However, this tilt should not change relative to the single unit made up of the shoulders, arms, hands and putter during the stroke.

A shoulder tilt at address will be influenced by the type of grip a golfer selects. For example, if the golfer has a left-hand-low grip the right shoulder may be slightly higher than the left.

Whatever the case we should lock the system such that

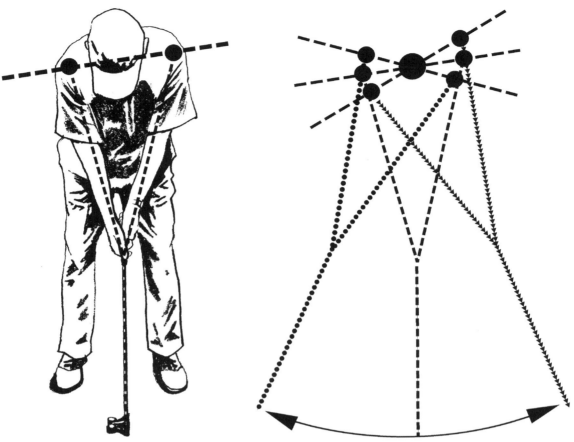

Lock and rock the system.

it becomes a single unit from the start of the back swing all the way through impact.

By working on the Lock and Rock of The System we:

a) Do not allow the wrists to break, which takes away any question about how much we should break the wrists for putts of varying lengths — a source of error.

b) Do not rotate the wrists as The System is moving in an inclined plane (to be discussed in the next chapter) which, relative to the ground and the vertical plane, will have a natural and defined rotation.

c) Do not allow the putter to move up or down because of the relatively straight arms fixing the distance from the axis of rotation to the putter head.

d) Do not move the arms without moving the shoulders and thus we maintain the arc throughout the stroke. The axis of rotation is the spine, with the pivot point close to the third thoracic vertebra between the upper portions of the shoulder blades.

If we do this — i.e. "Lock and Rock" the system — we don't allow the wrists to break (one DoF), we don't allow the wrists to rotate (another DoF) and we don't bend the arms while rocking the shoulders (another DoF). Thus, we have restrained these and minimized the errors associated with them.

One can thus understand that this fundamental is very important as it restrains rather than eliminates three Degrees of Freedom (DoF).

We can eliminate these three DoF by using a long putter: (1.), no up-and-down movement; (2.), no wrist break; and (3.), no rotation of the wrists.

So why are we not all playing with long putters? The reason is the same as why we are so good at throwing a basketball or a dart.

We need to admire how an expert dart player (thrower) or a professional basketball player — with a properly aligned stance — are able to manipulate their fingers, wrists, forearms, upper arms and shoulders to send a dart through the air to the bulls-eye, or swishing the basketball, by controlling all the DoF Mother Nature has provided.

If we eliminate some of these DoF by splinting an injured wrist we will certainly eliminate the source of error associated with an incorrect wrist break, but will also take the "feel" out of the throw. This will be the case until the splinted wrist is healed, or the dart thrower or basketball player practice enough to perfect the throw with a splint.

Yes, we may eventually adjust but it will be a handicap, which will place a ceiling on our potential to perform at our best. We need to control and restrain our DoF, not eliminate them.

We will address the long putter later and for those who

need one we will help demonstrate how to use it most effectively.

If we are aware of the need to minimize the DoF when applying the sixth Fundamental — i.e. "Lock and Rock" — we will be able to start making this movement without thinking while minimizing the sources or error.

Remember, there can be NO wrist break once you have initiated the backstroke, and NO arm or wrist rotation and NO bending of the arms but YES to a locked — not stiff, but relaxed — system, which includes the shoulders.

This system will be a single unit and able to move like a pendulum – even though it is NOT swinging in a vertical plane — as would the pendulum of a grandfather clock. The gravitational forces on this pendulum are almost the same as those on the pendulum of a clock, and these will influence the rhythm of the stroke, as we will discuss in Chapter Eight.

The locked system actually swings in a plane inclined at about 10 degrees to the vertical, which is the next and seventh Fundamental.

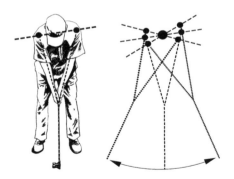

SUMMARY

Make sure we fix the system — shoulders, arms, wrists, hands and the putter — in place and rock it about the spine axis. This Lock and Rock fundamental will minimize the sources of error by restraining three DoF and thus minimize the sources of error associated with each.

THE SECRET:
"SWING PLANE
OF THE
PUTTING STROKE"

THIS IS NOT REALLY a secret because Mother Nature has prescribed it for every golfer who just lets it happen and wants to build confidence on the putting green. ¶ The problem is that there are some "Mother Nature Imposters" who have misinterpreted the prescription. They are influenced by what they think is happening, or a thought process that they employ to putt well themselves or what works for them. ¶ It seems that some putting experts don't fully understand the Fundamentals and how the body wants to function as they prescribe manipulated, contrived movements which have to be perfected so that they are reproduced very consistently from putt to putt — which requires many hours of practice — if the sources of error are to be minimized.

A report exposing the differences in the understanding of the basic movements of putting was reported in the August 2010 issue of *Golf Digest*. Here are quotes from this article that compared some of the better-known putting gurus on this particular aspect of the stroke, i.e. The Path:

GURU A: *"Straight wrist cock going back, right arm push going through"* and the path should be *"straight outside or inside going back, along the target line going through."*

GURU B: *"Dead-handed arm swing"* and the path should be *"straight back and straight through."*

GURU C: *"Shoulders turn, arms swing and forearms rotate"* and the path should be *"on an arc back and through."*

These quotes expose the different interpretations of what Mother Nature prescribes.

The swing plane is relatively easy to explain, but nowhere before has it been described and used effectively in putting instruction.

We started working on this aspect of the swing about 10 years ago while researching how to make the simplest and most efficient putting stroke.

If we understand the swing plane we will recognize how by employing it — allowing it to happen — in our putting stroke we can appropriately constrain selected DoF, thus minimizing the sources of error and effectively simplifying the putting stroke. We see this when we study and measure the kinematics of the swing.

We will — by adopting swing plane Fundamental No. 7 and the "Lock and Rock" Fundamental No. 6 — minimize the DoF, simplify the stroke and recognize that we are adopting a very natural kinematic movement.

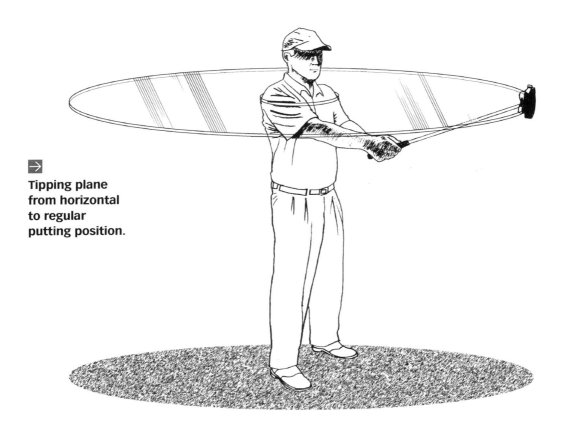

→

**Tipping plane
from horizontal
to regular
putting position.**

UNDERSTANDING THE SWING PLANE

L ET'S IMAGINE that a ball is hanging from your living
room ceiling, and you are standing erect with a putter in front of you (see the illustration above). Now
grip your putter as you normally would and position the putter head so it touches the ball. Your hands are below the ball
and putter head.

Now imagine there is a thin sheet (disc) of glass — a horizontal plane — parallel to the floor and about eight feet in
diameter, which goes through your body at a level just below
your shoulders, and centered at the third or fourth thoracic
vertebra. This imaginary disc of glass is the plane we will
refer to in this chapter.

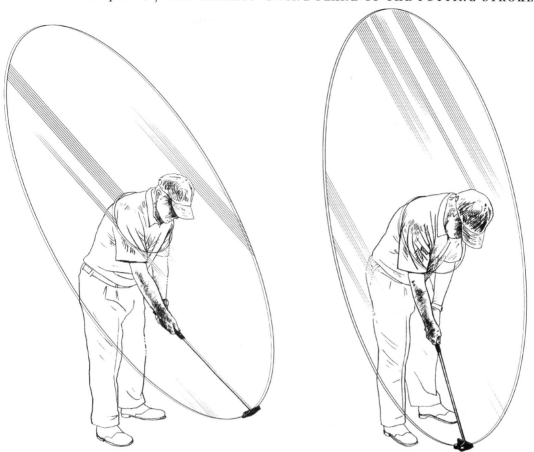

The System — i.e. the putter, arms, hands, wrists and shoulders — will rotate about the spine axis in this horizontal plane with the head of the putter staying in the plane.

In fact, the entire system rotates about the spine, and the putter-head path will describe a segment of a circle down onto the floor. The System remains fixed as it rotates about the spine.

This is important to understand because The System does not change within the plane as we tilt it over to 10 degrees to the vertical and into the putting posture (see illustration above).

When we tilt the plane over to the 10 degrees from the

vertical in the putting posture, and we look at the path projected down onto the green during a swing, it will describe a slight arc — a segment of an ellipse as it moves through the impact zone.

This is best seen in the following illustration from a bird's-eye view of the golfer in the putting position with the plane superimposed. You can see that a slight arc is described as viewed from above the golfer.

This is very important to understand because in the plane the putter doesn't rotate nor do the wrists break. In fact, The System remains in plane throughout the entire stroke and the orientation of the putter remains the same irrespective of where it is in the plane.

It's interesting that when swinging the putter in the 10-degree plane, the face RELATIVE to the ball will open on the back stroke and close through the stroke, AND will describe a slight arc through the impact zone BUT will not open or close in the 10-degree swing plane itself.

When we understand the swing plane we recognize how simple and natural the swing really is.

When we combine "The Swing Plane" Fundamental No. 7 with "Lock and Rock" Fundamental No. 6 — and you maintain the correct comfortable posture with weight evenly distributed on both feet throughout the stroke — the lower body will remain almost static during the stroke, thereby restraining or minimizing five DoF:

- *Up and down*
- *In and out*
- *Wrist break*
- *Wrist and forearm rotation*
- *Weight shift or sway*

The sixth DoF, ie. moving back and forth in the plane, we must have if we are to strike the ball.

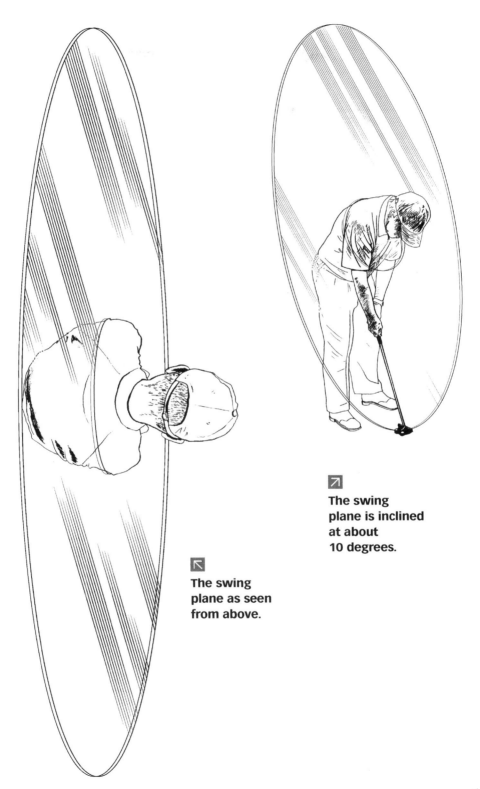

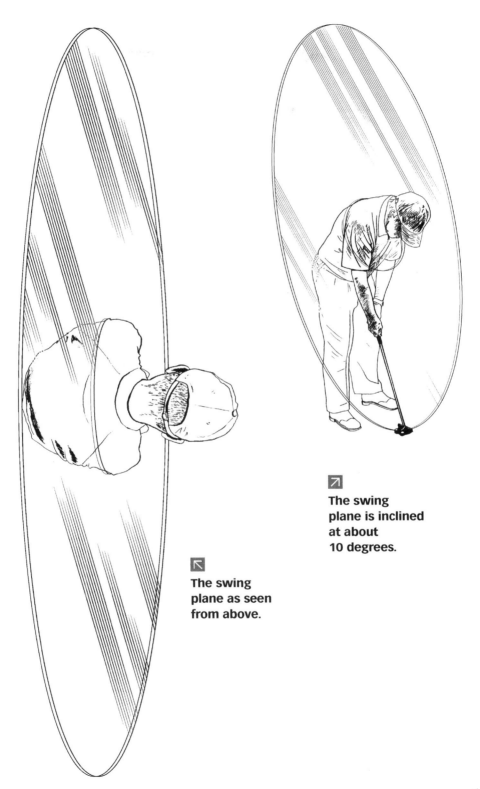
The swing
plane is inclined
at about
10 degrees.

The swing
plane as seen
from above.

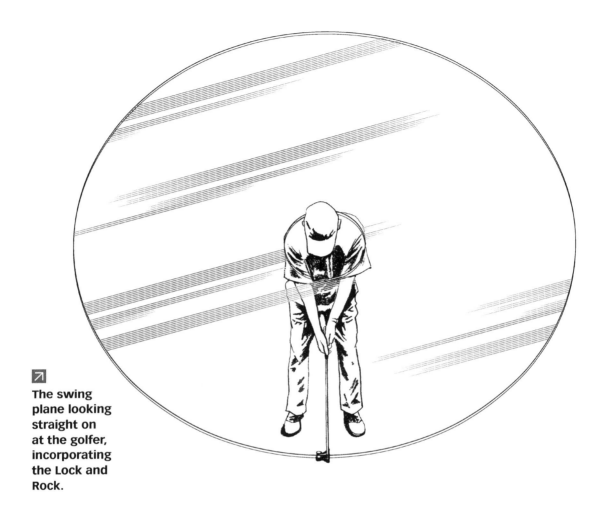

The swing plane looking straight on at the golfer, incorporating the Lock and Rock.

The swing plane is the secret that Mother Nature has prescribed. All we have to do is maintain a fixed system "Lock and Rock" and then "Let it Happen."

It is not complicated, and if we watch golfers who putt well we will observe these basic kinematics. In most cases they don't even know they are doing it. If they knew how important the swing plane is and understood its simplicity, they could tune up their strokes very quickly when experiencing putting stroke problems and inconsistencies. This would allow them to focus on other important things such as a good pre-shot routine, which we'll cover in Chapter 10.

Thank you Mother Nature.

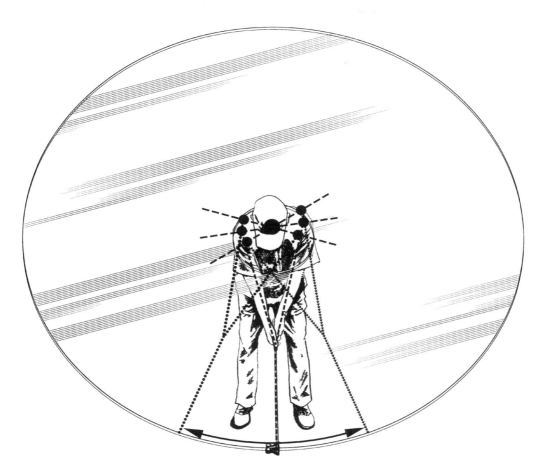

SUMMARY

Once you fix the system creating a single unit — with as little tension as possible to maintain the system in place and our eyes over the ball — then you must swing this system in a plane inclined at about 10 degrees to the vertical. Do not rotate or break the wrists. The putter head, when swinging in the plane, will describe an arc when projected on to the ground, and will open and close before and after the impact relative to the ball. Nothing changes within the plane.

FIND
YOUR
NATURAL
RHYTHM

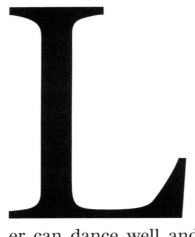

ET'S FIRST TALK about what we mean by "Rhythm." We don't mean that the golfer can dance well and can tap his/her feet in time with the music. We mean he/she has found and can maintain the same timing or tempo of the stroke for all putts. ¶ A natural rhythm will build consistency into your stroke and minimize the sources of error in the back and forth DoF (Degree of Freedom). ¶ One of the biggest problems that most golfers have — even tour players — is bad rhythm. Many golfers refer to this as tempo. However, in this chapter we will refer to the phenomenon as "Rhythm" and we discuss how to find YOUR natural rhythm.

FINDING YOUR NATURAL RHYTHM

L ET'S ASSUME FOR A MINUTE that the shoulders, arms, hands and putter are a single fixed unit. If this unit is allowed to swing freely (as in the case of a child in a swing) when pivoted about a point between the shoulders it will have a specific rhythm (frequency).

This is very close to the rhythm with which we should putt for all putts, be they short putts or long putts — within reason.

One way to find a good rhythm close to the natural frequency of your pendulum-like system (your shoulders, arms, hands and putter) is to putt a number of balls with one hand. Make sure that you don't bend your elbow or your wrist, and that your arm remains relatively straight. We suggest that you use your right hand if you are right handed.

It is very important when putting with one hand that you only have enough grip pressure to support the putter through the putting arc. Don't try to hit the ball, which will require an increase in grip pressure. Let the putter do all the work for you.

This one-handed putting rhythm will be close to the correct rhythm for you. When you are getting close to a good one-handed rhythm you will know it, as the impact will feel soft and sweet.

Once you feel so comfortable putting with one hand that you seriously start thinking about using this style of putting for real, you are ready to place the other hand on the putter. Just let the other hand go along for the ride and to help stabilize the putter through the swing.

This one-handed technique gets you into the ballpark of the correct rhythm and close to what you should use for all putts.

Another way to get a feel for this rhythm is to stand upright and swing a putter at your side, forward and back like a pendulum, with a straight arm. Don't break your wrists or bend your elbow. You will find a natural rhythm if you have very little pressure gripping the club or even holding the putter between two fingers.

This rhythm is so natural that we don't have to think about it nor do we have to try to control it. We can talk on our cell phone (not too loudly) or even read a book while the pendulum (our arm and the putter) is swinging back and forth. The complete cycle of this swing will be about two seconds.

**One-handed
putting is
excellent
practice to
help you
find your
rhythm.**

To appreciate the timing of this natural rhythm, try to double the frequency to one second for a complete cycle. You will find that a lot of effort is required with a very firm grip as well as a lot of concentration in trying to maintain the one-second cycle rhythm.

While making a proper putting stroke, allow your shoulders, arms, hands and putter (a single unit) to swing freely back and forth, with a rhythm very similar to the one-handed putt. This will come naturally as long as you do not grip the putter as if you were choking it. A light grip is essential in combination with no tension in your arms.

REPEAT YOUR RHYTHM

W E NEED TO UNDERSTAND that when putting, we STROKE the ball, not STRIKE it. Many golfers believe that they have to calculate how hard to "hit" the ball on the green, based on their distance from the hole. This is not a conscious calculation but an intuitive motion based on subconsciously processed information.

In fact, the rhythm of the stroke should remain constant for long and short putts. The only difference is the distance we take the putter back. This becomes intuitive, as is the case when

throwing a ball to someone at different distances from you.

If we go to an example of a child in a swing, the higher you push the child to initiate the free swinging motion, the faster the child's feet will pass over the ground at the lowest part of the swing path.

In putting this means that the putter head will move faster the farther back you take it on the backstroke while staying with your Rhythm.

By doing this, you will start to see much more consistency in the distance control of your putts. Putting also becomes easier because once you find your rhythm you are not concerned about how hard to hit each putt.

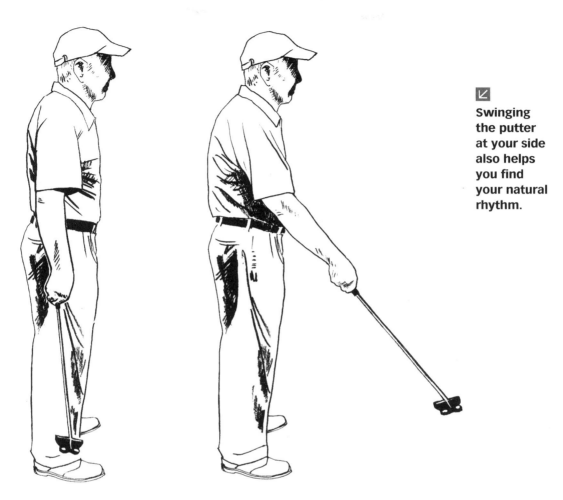

Swinging the putter at your side also helps you find your natural rhythm.

WHY IS MY RHYTHM DIFFERENT THAN THAT OF MY FRIEND?

I F I AM TALL AND HAVE LONG, muscular arms and they are relatively straight when making a stroke, and my putter is fairly long, my pendulum (system) will be heavier than my friend's, who has shorter, thinner arms and a shorter putter. All this weight (mass) is spread out over the length of the system away from the axis or pivot point between the shoulder blades.

For this reason, the natural frequency (Rhythm) of my system is going to be slower than that of my friend — not much, but it will be different — which means we have a different Natural Rhythm.

THE PHYSICS OF NATURAL RHYTHM

N OW YOU KNOW HOW to find your natural rhythm, and why your natural rhythm may be different from that of your friend.

For those of you who want more information, we will cover in more depth some of the basic physics.

As we discussed earlier, rhythm is dictated by the natural frequency of the fixed unit — pendulum or The System — made up of the shoulders, arms, wrists, hands and putter all remaining in the same position relative to each other throughout the stroke. This is the "Lock and Rock" described in Chapter Six.

This fixed unit or pendulum has a natural frequency. "Rhythm" is dictated by the Moment of Inertia — mass distribution about a defined pivot point — of the system (pendulum). This frequency is very much the same within small angles — 45-degrees or less, back and forth. An example is the rhythm or frequency of a clock's pendulum swinging through its back-and-forth cycle.

If we want to change the frequency "rhythm" of a clock pendulum — to make it go faster or slower — we must decrease or increase the weight of the "bob" OR decrease or increase the bob's distance from the axis of rotation or the pivot point.

The number of beats a minute — the frequency of the pendulum — is almost the same, irrespective of the distance it moves, when the total angle through which it swings is less than about 90 degrees. Just like a child in a swing, the number of swings per minute — once you let the child swing freely — is almost the same no matter how high, within reason, you push the child to start the motion.

With this in mind let's consider the rhythm of a putting stroke. The fixed unit, which we call the "pendulum," does not actually swing in a vertical plane like that of a clock — but in a plane at about 10 degrees to the vertical (see Chapter

Seven: Swing Plane). However, it still has the characteristic of a clock pendulum based on its mass distribution.

Having said this I am now going to muddy the waters a little by telling you (but I want you to forget it immediately thereafter) that the putting stroke as the putter head approaches the ball is constantly accelerating — very slightly — from the top of the back swing all the way to impact. BUT this is something we do not need to be concerned with, as we seem to do it intuitively without trying.

The reason why you should forget about this acceleration is that if you think about it AND/OR try to accelerate the putter head, you will soon be outside of your natural Frequency Zone (Rhythm) and start punching the ball – i.e. "striking" it instead of "stroking" it.

Again, we need to understand that we do not use the putter by swinging it back and forth all the way through a cycle like a pendulum. We start from a dead stop at address and take it back to the full extent of the backstroke, then allow gravity to help move it forward to impact — with a very small amount of acceleration which we don't have to think about. The ratio of time for the backstroke to the time of the forward stroke is about 2:1.

Find this rhythm during your pre-shot routine (Chapter 10) by swinging the club back and forth, which is sometimes referred to as practice swings. This rhythm is what we need to maintain for every length of putt.

Don't be a "Jerk" — not in the sense of a nasty person but a golfer who "Jerks" the putter back and "Punches" the forward stroke. This is what leads to inconsistencies in distance control and introduces sources of error. Even the best golfers cannot do this the same way each time over a wide range of putts. Take the putter back and let the gravitational forces help you bring it forward naturally.

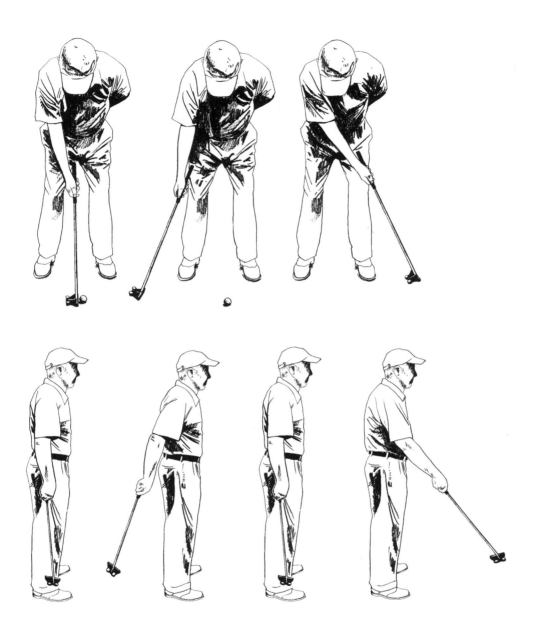

SUMMARY

**You have a natural rhythm based on the pendulum (single unit) you
have created — shoulders, arms, wrists, hands and putter — and
to find this rhythm practice putting with one hand with a straight
arm, fixed wrist and a very light grip. Don't fight your natural
rhythm, and make sure you have the same rhythm for every putt.**

9

WHAT SHOULD YOU BE LOOKING AT, WHY & WHEN?

I F YOU HAVE WANDERING EYES, you will probably get into trouble off the course, but certainly on the course, including developing bad habits when putting. ¶ What do you look at when you are putting? Do you watch the ball? Or the putter head? The path of your stroke? You might not even be aware where you are looking or what you are looking at. Once you have read this chapter you will understand the importance of controlling what you look at and when.

There has been a significant amount of research conducted on eye movement during the act of putting by Dr. Joan Vickers of the University of Calgary in Canada, a member of our advisory board.

This work involves studying what golfers of different skill levels look at just before and while making a putt. Using eye-tracking technology allowing her to view what the golfer is looking at, Vickers discovered that low-handicap golfers have what she calls "Quiet Eye [QE]" defined as a fixation held stable on the top or back of the ball for two to three seconds prior to and during the putting stroke."

Drawing from this, and other research, let's "focus" on what we should be looking at:

1. YOUR EYES provide the information the mind processes, and sends subconscious messages to the body to perform an act. In putting this includes the distance, direction and path the ball must follow to sink the putt.

2. AFTER COMPLETING the Preparation phase of your Pre-Shot Routine and having an image of the path of the ball, position yourself so your eyes are directly above the ball.

3. AIM THE PUTTER HEAD at the target point, ensuring correct putter head alignment.

4. SET YOUR STANCE correctly.

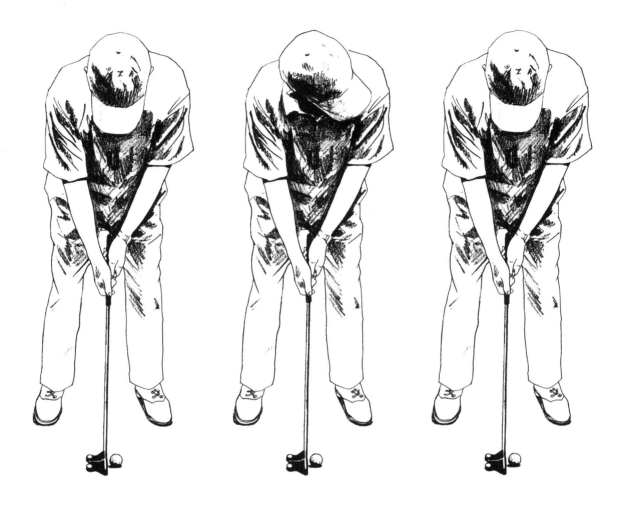

5. NOW IT'S TIME to connect to the hole by looking at a point — within approximately 12 inches of the hole — over which the ball will travel on its way into the hole.

6. LOOK AT THIS POINT and back to the ball a couple of times until you feel connected.

7. VERY IMPORTANT: Now focus your eyes on the contact point between the putter face and the ball before impact, and on a spot below this point during and for several seconds or more after impact.

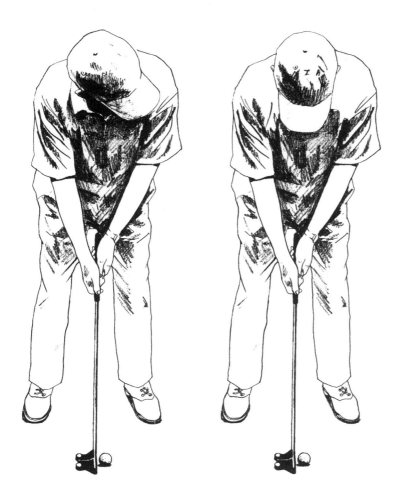

Take a couple of looks to connect to the hole.

All these steps are important. However, let's discuss Step Nos. 2 and 7 in a little more detail.

In Step No. 2, positioning the eyes directly over the ball in the target-line/ball plane will give you the ability to set up with the putter properly aligned, looking down the line and directly over it.

Some golfers prefer to position the eyes just inside of the ball/target-line plane, but tests show this is not good and difficult to replicate consistently. Trying to judge "a little bit off" is not as consistent as judging "directly on," i.e. directly over the ball. For example, as previously mentioned, if you decided to set up with your eyes — to exaggerate and make the point — two feet inside the ball/target-line plane, it would be difficult to align yourself properly as you wouldn't be looking down the line but trying to judge it from the side.

Step No. 7 is crucial to good putting.

This means your eyes — quiet eyes [QE] — remain absolutely still from the beginning to the end of the stroke. Vickers' research reveals:

"The onset of this eye focus of elite putters begins about a second before the backstroke, lasts for one second throughout the stroke, but most important of all stays rock solid on the green [a spot on the green just behind where the ball lay before impact] for about a half-second or more AFTER the ball leaves the putter face."

Looking up too soon upsets your stroke and almost always results in moving out of the swing plane just before impact, in most cases resulting in a disappointing missed putt. This is especially true for short putts, where the temptation to look up to see if the ball goes in the hole is greatest.

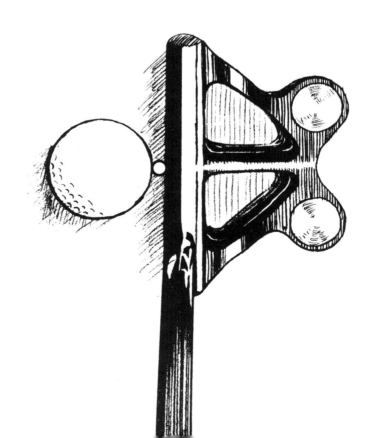

Keep your eyes focused on a spot behind the ball (see dot).

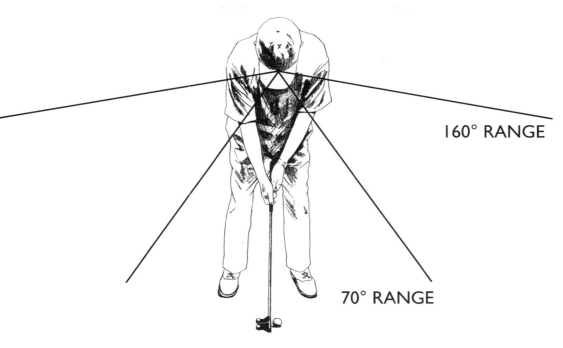

160° RANGE

70° RANGE

Over the years, we have all heard the old adage "Don't look up." We all know — but some of us don't believe — that we have no influence over the path of the ball after it has left the putter face, no matter how much we talk to the ball or body English we use. Looking up will not help and, in almost all cases, hurts.

Controlling our peripheral vision is important when putting.

PERIPHERAL VISION

IF WE HAVE reasonably good eyesight, we will have peripheral vision, which allows us to sense things around us even though we are not looking directly at them. This wide-angle peripheral vision (approximately 160 degrees in humans) is very important to us if we do not want to trip over the curb or step in a hole, etc.

It also helps if someone or something is approaching you from one side or another and you are likely to collide. Your peripheral vision will see this problem immediately and pass the information on to the brain. In milliseconds (about 150 or less) a signal is sent to those parts of your body able to take some evasive action to avoid the collision.

Unfortunately, this peripheral vision can be a detriment when putting – especially if you have a Type-"A" personality and want to be in total control of everything you do.

The reason for this is that being Type "A" you are probably more aware and feel the need to react to things around you than others who are not. As a result, you may sense the path of the head — within a range of approximately 70 degrees (plus or minus 35 degrees from where you are looking), where our peripheral vision can distinguish objects fairly clearly. You may perceive this path to be too slow, too fast, too far off line, etc., and then subconsciously react to make an "in-flight" correction.

This interference with your natural stroke causes swing-path problems and some mental conflict. To offset the natural reaction viewed in the peripheral vision we need to attentively focus on the spot behind the ball during the stroke (Quiet Eye).

Tests have shown that peripheral vision can, in some cases, help on short putts of three feet or less. The reason for this is that you can maintain your focus on the spot behind the ball (Quiet Eye) while having the hole in your peripheral view.

Because most golfers want to see the hole they shift their eyes off the ball to bring the hole into their peripheral view. This throws their whole stroke off. The golfer often doesn't know why and, indeed, is unaware that he/she is doing this.

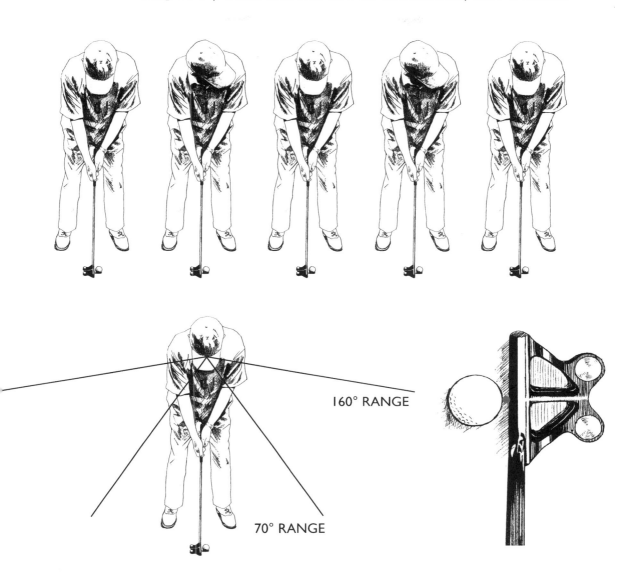

160° RANGE

70° RANGE

SUMMARY

Imagine the shot during the pre-shot routine, then address the ball. Now aim the putter head at the Target Point along the target line. Connect to the hole by looking at a point — within approximately 12 inches of the hole — over which the ball will travel on its way into the hole. Look at this point and back to the ball a couple of times until you feel connected. Now, focus your eyes on a spot between the back of the ball and the clubface before, during and, for several seconds or more, after impact.

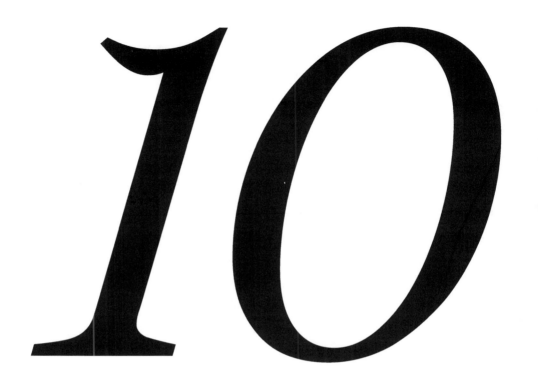

10

PLANNING

&

PRE-SHOT

ROUTINE

E OFTEN TALK TO our students about the similarities between the problems we face in life and business, and the challenges we face on the putting green. You must properly identify the challenge, make a plan to overcome it and then prepare to execute your plan, choosing to believe you can make the putt. ¶ If you know you don't have a structured and systematic approach to making your plan, are unsure of the challenge or how you need to prepare to execute your plan, you will not be able to develop the needed confidence in knowing that everything is in order and you are ready to pull the trigger. As a result your putting performance will be inconsistent.

The planning and pre-shot routines are two elements of the preparation you need to putt effectively. It requires confidence in your plan as well as the mental and physical ability to let it happen. There is NO ROOM FOR DOUBT when you are over the ball.

A Pre-Shot Routine should follow a consistent series of steps. What's important is that we not only follow the physical steps, but also the mental steps.

Dr. Debbie Crews, a leading researcher and expert in this area, identified many years ago that top players' routines take a specific amount of time after doing it so often.

However, as Dr. Crews points out, we should not aspire to make sure that our routine lasts for "x" seconds. Rather, if we follow our process consistently, and trust our mental and physical steps, the number of seconds it takes will be approximately the same.

We have amazing intuitive abilities and we need to trust them.

To better understand how great our abilities really are, let's use an example such as throwing a golf ball to someone located five feet from us, and then again after they move about 20 feet away from us. We seem to be able to do this without pause or calculation of the distance — we do not count the number of steps the person takes backward away from us, we just process the information based on what we see and just do it.

We have a choice of either turning our putting into a mindless mechanical process using charts, tables, maps and other devices to help provide the information to make the correct movements – a very complex robotic process which we are not very efficient at doing — or rely on our abilities, athletic intuition and visual senses based on what we observe.

"Your gaze actually works as a GPS system," Dr. Vickers suggests. "It is naturally attuned to the environment you are in and, if you give your visual system the time to actually see the problem that needs to be solved, your brain and body will carry out the plan you devise. Rob your visual system and brain of the time it needs and it will work no better than a poorly programmed GPS."

We are going to deal with the planning and pre-shot routine separately. First is planning what you want to do, and the second part is preparing to do it and, finally, doing it.

PART ONE: PLANNING WHAT TO DO

1. Understand the Challenge

Your ball is on the green some distance from the hole and your challenge is to get the ball into the hole in the fewest number of strokes.

2. Find a Solution

Quantify the variables based on what you see and what your feet and body feel, using the putting ability that you have acquired, and your experience.

The variables you should consider are:

a) Distance of the putt

b) Speed of the green

c) Speed of the putt

d) Path of the putt based on the slope of the green and the fall line and a), b) and c) above.

A specific process for reading the green will be described in Chapter 11 (The Fundamentals of Green Reading).

PART TWO: PRE-SHOT ROUTINE

THIS IS WHEN YOU NEED to follow a very specific routine, by mentally building an image and feel of what you intend to do by looking at the hole and swinging the club to develop the rhythm of the motion you intend to use.

Building this image and physically preparing and feeling what is about to happen is the final preparation stage.

At this point in the process, having taken all the variables in the Planning Phase into account, the pre-shot routine starts as we prepare to both mentally and physically execute the putt.

We need to call on and trust our abilities and visual system, and prepare to switch from an analytical thought process to a well-practiced and auto-pilot mindset.

1. We recommend that you stand behind the ball looking at the target — some golfers prefer to stand alongside it, which is fine. Look at the hole while preparing to make the stroke by swinging the putter back and forth with your natural rhythm, and imagine the path of the putt.

As you swing the putter with a natural rhythm, you will be developing a feel for how far back the putter will need to go without trying to calculate it. Just the same way you were able to throw a ball to a distant or nearby target.

This movement of the putter head should not be considered a practice stroke but rather a rhythmic swing simulating the tempo you are about to use, developing a "feel" for the putt. We will call this a "feel swing" from here onwards.

In this stage you are bringing together the image of the ball traveling to the hole and the feel of the stroke you are about to make with the putter.

It may take one, two or more swings to get the feeling, but as soon as you are ready, commit to making the stroke.

2. This is the final stage of your pre-shot routine after you have committed to, and are ready to make the stroke.

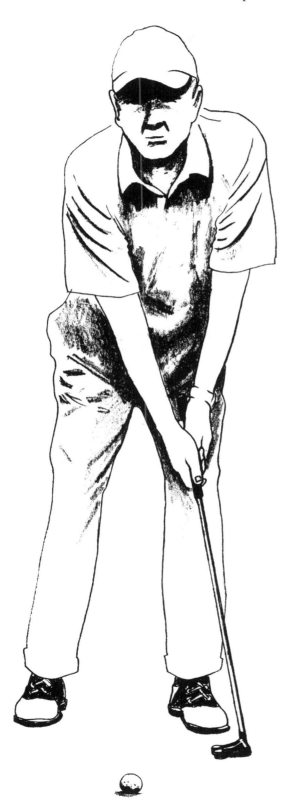

 Look at the hole while finding your rhythm and feel.

Now you are ready to make the putt and move the thought process from the "analytical" side of your brain to the "auto-pilot" side just before striking the ball.

This will look familiar from Chapter Nine, but we recommend following these steps as part of your Pre-Shot Routine:

a) Position yourself such that your eyes are directly over the ball.

EYES
DIRECTLY
ABOVE BALL

Eyes over the ball.

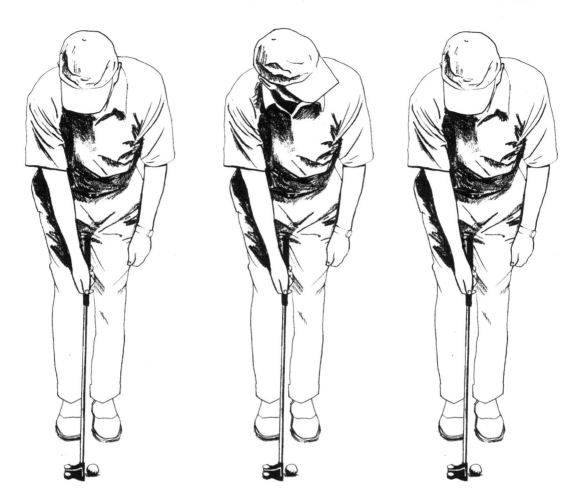

b) Aim the putter head at the target point, along the target line, to ensure proper alignment.

Be sure to aim the putter head carefully.

c)   Set your stance

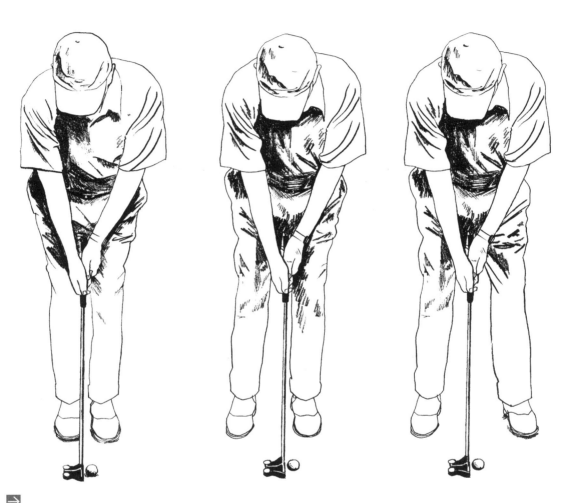

→
Take your stance.

d) Now it's time to connect to the hole by looking at a point — within approximately 12 inches of the hole — over which the ball will travel on its way into the hole.

e) Look at this point and then back to the ball a couple of times until you feel connected.

Connect to
the hole.

f) VERY IMPORTANT: Now focus your eyes on a spot between the back of the ball and the clubface before, during and for several seconds or more after impact.

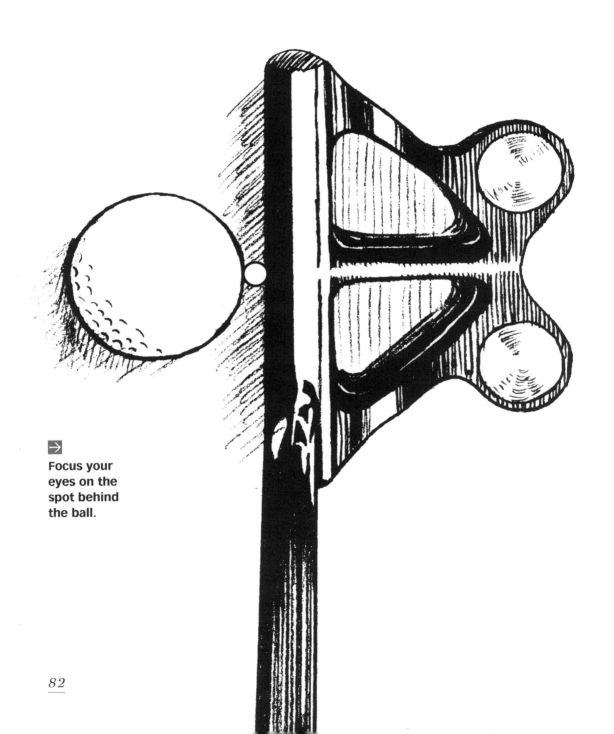

Focus your
eyes on the
spot behind
the ball.

We need to practice this routine and remember that every routine is individual, based on your preference and what is most successful for you. This is an overall template that may be adapted and tweaked by the individual.

For example, in (d) some golfers may find it hard to identify a point within 12 inches of the hole and will instead prefer to connect with a point "x" number of balls to the left or right of the hole.

The key is to follow both the physical and mental steps consistently.

This final stage should become automatic with practice. However, to help you remember what you need to do, think about having a nice P-A-C-E to your routine:

P-osition

A-im

C-onnect

E-yes

If at anytime while over the ball, you have any doubts about the line or distance, or if there is ANY CONFLICT in your mind, STOP and repeat Step Nos. 1 and 2.

One of the most common causes of conflict we have found in working with all levels of golfers is using the line on the ball as an aim line.

AIM LINE ON THE BALL

BECAUSE TIGER and some other elite golfers use and aim a line on the ball to line up with the target, many golfers believe it is going to help them. However, research has yet to show that using a line on a ball helps players sink more putts.

We suggest that you don't use the aim-line on the ball to identify the target line. In fact, we try to stop golfers from this practice, even the tour pros who visit us to get help with their putting.

Very few golfers are capable of doing this correctly and even if they were it does not seem to make a difference, other than possibly some mental comfort, which may help if it is done correctly. The down side of using a line on the ball to aim the putt is not worth the potential problems it can cause.

We have found that a miss-aligned aim-line on a ball will become apparent to a good golfer as soon as they are over the ball. In many cases, even when they know it, they will not try to realign the ball for various reasons, such as "I can handle it," "I don't want to hold up play," "I am wasting time" or "I may get a warning for slow play."

The perceived miss-alignment of the aim-line causes conflict, which we discussed above and is something we don't need, when attempting a putt.

SUMMARY

Analyze the situation and develop a solution to the challenge that you face on the green. Then prepare to implement your solution. This preparation should be very similar each time. Create an image of what you expect to happen and develop a feel (rhythm) for the stroke, bringing together the image and feel. Now, position yourself over the ball, aim the putter head at your target point, connect and finally focus your eyes on the contact point between the putter and the ball for several seconds after impact.

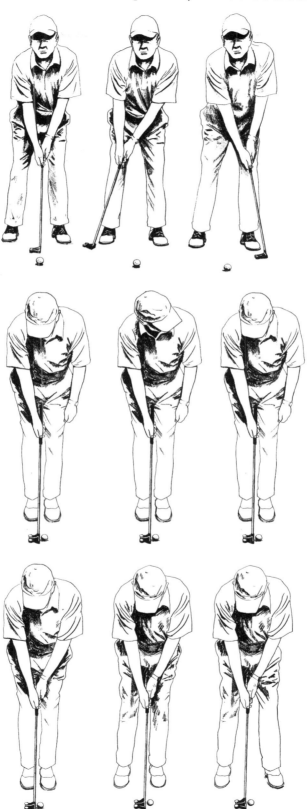

11

THE
FUNDAMENTALS
OF
GREEN READING

B

EFORE WE DISCUSS the all-important Fall Line we need to understand what factors will influence the way a ball will travel on the green such as:

- the slope(s);
- up and downhill;
- overall undulations between the ball and the hole;
- the distance from the ball to the hole;
- the speed of the green.

Once we have quantified and included each of these factors in our mental calculations we will have all the information we need to make a good putt. Easy, isn't it?

The ability to read a green is dependent on our experience and acquired abilities. This skill is learned and improves with experience, but we can do with a little help to shorten the learning curve. However, we still need to understand how to interpret what we see.

What we should avoid is turning green-reading into a mechanical process. If we become overly reliant on devices, tables and charts to read greens we will not develop our natural ability based on the processed information provided by our visual observation to perform this function.

If our visual observation tells us something different from the charts and table values, we will be mentally conflicted. This is something we do not need when we are over the ball, ready to make a putt.

Simply because the technology is available does not mean we need it or should use it.

However, we do need to understand certain physical laws, which will affect how the ball rolls on the green, allowing our natural abilities to play their part more effectively.

Several physicists have studied and reported on the trajectory of a ball rolling on a green. They have explained, in general terms, what happens when a ball is rolling on a green and why the ball breaks the way it does.

What these physicists tell us is not outside of what makes intuitive sense to us, and certainly helps us better understand what our visual observations and experience tell us — thus giving us the confidence we need to plan our putt.

These learned men include H.A. Templeton, who discusses these issues in his book, "Vector Putting," Frank Werner in his book, "Better Golf From New Research," and Robert Grober in his paper on "The Geometry of Putting On a Planar Surface," which revisits some of Templeton's work. We will discuss some of their research later.

All three of these researchers have used and made frequent reference to the "Stimpmeter" readings to identify one of the most important factors in green reading, i.e. the speed of the green (read more about the story of the Stimpmeter in the Appendix).

As we now proceed through this chapter, we will discuss only what we need to know to help us sink more putts and not encumber ourselves with "stuff" we really don't need to know at this stage, which will only complicate matters.

THE FALL LINE

As PREVIOUSLY MENTIONED, to read a green you need to assess the situation regarding the topography of the green — slopes, up/downhill, undulations, etc. — having first calibrated yourself with regard to the speed of the green based on several putts on the practice putting green. The speed on the practice green should be the same speed as the greens on the course.

Second, you need to find the FALL LINE around the hole. If the slopes are different over the path the ball will be traveling then we need to take these into account as well.

The Fall Line on a green is the line along which a ball will travel in a straight line and have no break due to the forces of gravity. It is easy to find on severe slopes but as the slope gets less severe, the fall line becomes more difficult to see.

If you roll a ball at a hole, which is on a slope, from different positions you will find a point from which it will not veer off line as it moves directly down (or up) the slope at the hole. This is the Fall Line.

Intuitively we understand this, so it is nothing new. In green reading, however, it is very important to establish where the Fall Line is around the hole, and know that every putt —

whether it's uphill or downhill — will break towards this line.

Knowing that the ball from any position around the hole will break toward the Fall Line is very helpful. The degree to which it will break will be dependent on the slope, but the maximum break around the hole will be at right angles to the Fall Line (in the following illustration, ball Nos. 3 and 9) and minimum break — i.e. no break — will be directly up or down the Fall Line (in the following illustration, ball Nos. 12 and 7).

Understand the Fall Line and the Target Point.

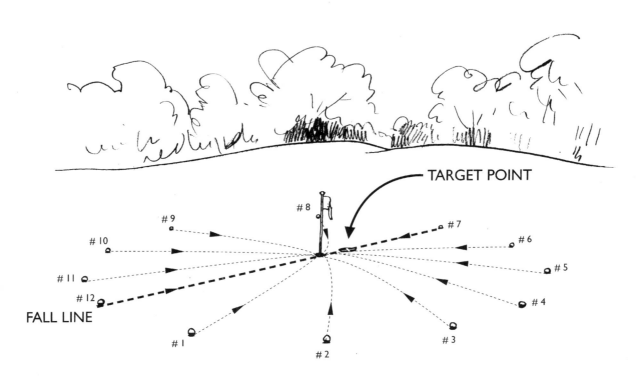

TARGET POINT

FALL LINE

STEPS TO FOLLOW WHEN YOU READ A GREEN

THIS PROCESS will help determine the break on your putts within 10 to 15 feet from the hole, assuming that the slope is about the same (planar) in the area over which you will be putting.

1. Find the Fall Line.

2. Position yourself at 90 degrees to the Fall Line to determine the maximum break.

3. Imagine how a ball will break from this maximum break-point position and select a Target Point at which to aim (assuming this ball is the same distance from the hole as your ball).

4. Move to your ball and use this same Target Point selected in No. 3 above to aim your putt as you go through your Pre-Shot Routine.

So, to summarize: First you find the Fall Line, then move to a point at 90 degrees to that line and select a Target Point. Move to your ball and aim at that same Target Point (the target line).

"How can this possibly work?" I hear you ask.

Well, I previously mentioned Robert Grober's work, which proves that, assuming the slope is constant (planar) around the hole, all putts from the same distance have a single Target Point which is on the Fall Line.

This will obviously make sense if you conduct the following experiment:

Find the Target Point as in No. 3 above and insert a tee in the ground at this point. Now move around the hole, viewing this Target Point from various positions around the compass. You will note that as you approach the Fall Line the target line gets closer to the edge of the hole.

What is essential in green reading is to determine your Target Point (the line along which you should aim your putter) and putt directly at it, as if it were a straight putt along

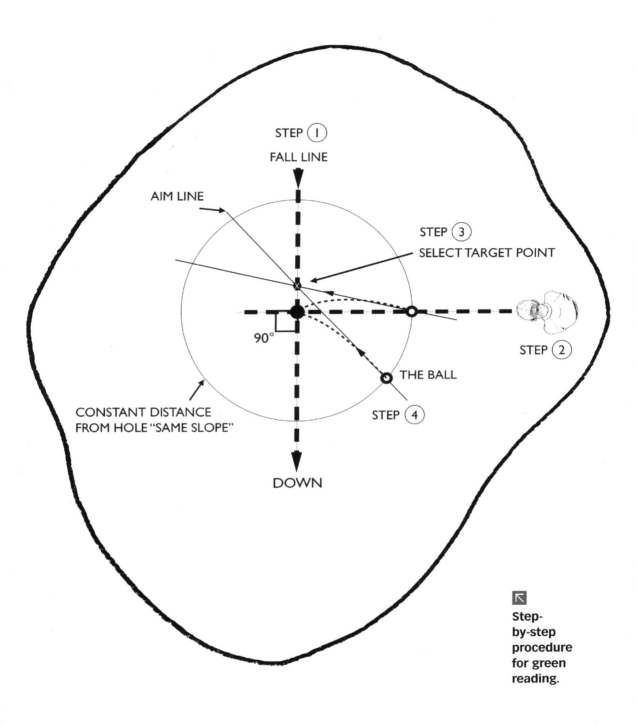

STEP ① FALL LINE

AIM LINE

STEP ③ SELECT TARGET POINT

90°

STEP ②

THE BALL

STEP ④

CONSTANT DISTANCE FROM HOLE "SAME SLOPE"

DOWN

Step-by-step procedure for green reading.

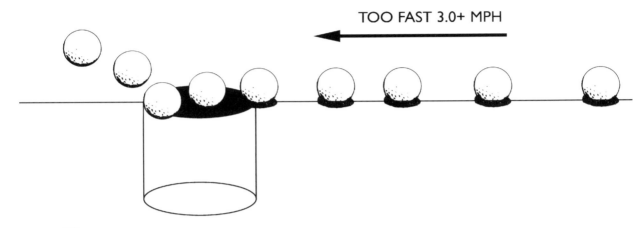

TOO FAST 3.0+ MPH

Fast, off center putts will lip out at 3.5 mph. Even online putts will hit the back lip and bounce over the hole.

that line. Most golfers think they should putt at the apex (top of or the highest point of the curve) of the breaking path. Aiming at the apex is one of the reasons why most of us miss putts on the low side, as we do not often start the putt on the target line.

We don't need to know too much more when we are reading greens. But we do need to practice finding the Fall Line and the Target Point to aim at by putting across the slope and getting a good feel for how the putt will break from 90 degrees to the Fall Line and then keep this Target Point in mind when putting from different positions around the hole. Obviously, the speed at which you putt is critical.

When you are ready to putt having done all the analysis based on what you observe — i.e. subconsciously processed the information — then, as is the case when you throw a ball, just Let it Happen.

WHY DO PUTTS BREAK?

THE REASON FOR a ball following a parabolic curve (more break at the end of the putt than when it starts) on its way to the hole is because of what is called "precession" (don't worry). This is the same phenom-

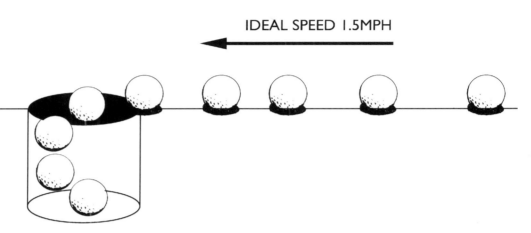

IDEAL SPEED 1.5MPH

enon which allows you to ride your bike without holding the handlebars. As the bike tilts sideways to the left, the wheel steers to the left.

If you have ever held a spinning bicycle wheel by the axle and tried to tilt it — left hand downward and right hand up — it will actually turn to the left rather than tilt.

Similarly, as a tilting force is applied to the ball on a slope — the sideways force due to the ball's center of gravity not being directly over the contact point on the green — the rolling ball will turn to the left. When the ball slows down the sideways force remains the same so the ball will turn faster.

We have all experienced this during the last couple of rotations of a putt when the ball seems to take a dive left or right.

This is not good and we want to avoid this dying break as the amount of break is unpredictable – so don't try to die the ball into the hole.

To take this variable out of the mix try to get the ball to enter the hole at optimum speed. This speed is about 1.5 mph, best thought of as the ball hitting the back wall of the cup.

Faster, off-center putts — such as 3.0 mph —will lip out and straight, on-line putts at 3.5 mph will hit the back lip and bounce over the hole.

At the optimum speed we avoid the last-second precession dive and will hole more putts. Thus, try to stroke putts

↖

Optimum speed for a putt is 1.5 mph, best thought of as the ball hitting the back wall of the cup.

that reach the hole at a speed where they hit the back wall of the cup upon entry, rather than tottering and turning as they die at the hole.

EVERY PUTT STARTS BY SKIDDING, SLIDING THEN ROLLING

IF YOU HAVE EVER PLAYED pool you will have noticed that the cushions surrounding the table are not situated at the same height as the center of the pool ball but approximately two-thirds up the diameter of the ball (center of percussion of the ball). This is to make sure that the ball bounces back with pure rolling spin and does not bounce over the cushion.

To get pure rolling spin on a pool ball (or golf ball on a green) one needs to strike the ball – make contact between the ball and the putter face traveling horizontally — at a point opposite its center of percussion. This is a little more than one inch above the ground level for a golf ball, which would mean that you need a negative loft of a little more than 15 degrees OR, with no loft on the putter, a rise angle of 15-plus degrees.

Neither of these two options actually works when putting.

For this reason – and to get the ball consistently out of the depression in which it will inevitably sit – we need about four degrees of loft on the putter. If the club is moving horizontally or has a little rise angle — which we recommend — the ball will always have a little (very little) backspin and be launched off the ground. It will then touch down and start skidding until the friction between the ball and the green's surface gets it into a pure rolling mode.

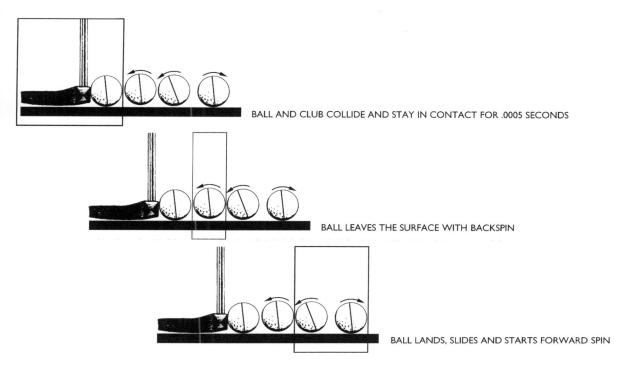

BALL AND CLUB COLLIDE AND STAY IN CONTACT FOR .0005 SECONDS

BALL LEAVES THE SURFACE WITH BACKSPIN

BALL LANDS, SLIDES AND STARTS FORWARD SPIN

DISTANCE BEFORE PURE ROLLING SPIN STARTS IS ≈15% OF PUTT DISTANCE

The distance from where the ball leaves the putter face to where it gets pure rolling is about 15 percent of the distance of the putt. This distance is less than 15 percent if the loft on the putter is two degrees, but not much less.

Understand what happens after impact.

SHORT PUTTS

CONSIDERING THAT THE BALL takes about 15 percent of the putt's distance to get rolling spin and that on a two-foot putt which, for optimum speed, should go about one foot past the hole, this makes the effective length of this putt about three feet, of which just over five inches is skidding, etc. Thus, the only chance the putt can be affected by the break is the 19 inches before it reaches the hole.

We suggest that the optimum speed of about 1.5 mph as the ball approaches the hole — slower for downhill putts on faster greens — will take out most of the last-minute diving break on short putts, so don't aim outside the hole on two-foot putts and putt it with confidence. Keep your head and eyes down, and listen for the ball falling in the hole.

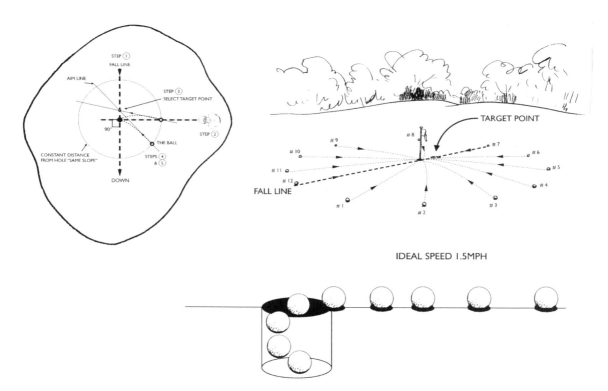

IDEAL SPEED 1.5MPH

SUMMARY

Find the Fall Line, estimate the break from a similar-length putt but at right angles to the Fall Line, select a Target Point and aim along this target line as if it was a straight putt. Remember that your putt should travel at a sufficient pace so it will hit the back wall of the cup. Don't expect to make every putt but believe you can.

QUICK

REFERENCE

SUMMARY

THIS CHAPTER'S EXISTENCE does not imply that it should be used for anything other than a reference and reminder of the fundamentals and the sequence in which each must be addressed. We need to refer back to the text if there is anything you have forgotten or you are not sure about, and remember to practice with a purpose. ¶ We also invite you to visit www.franklygolf.com for some very helpful hints, drills, tests and other useful information to help you improve and have more fun practicing.

PART ONE: THE FUNDAMENTALS OF PUTTING

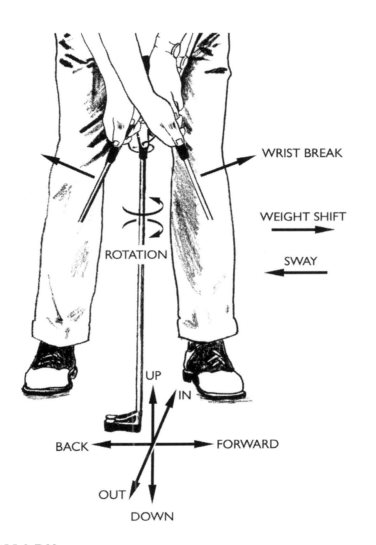

The Six
Degrees of
Freedom

SUMMARY
Knowing and understanding the six DoF — and applying
the fundamentals — will minimize their effect and the
sources of error associated with each, leading to greater
consistency in our putting.

CHAPTER ONE
Diagnose Your Putting Skills

SUMMARY
Identify and define your weaknesses and rate your putting skills, then go about working to strengthen these and work diligently on those areas that need the most help. Once you have read the book and applied the teachings you need to return to this page and again rate your putting skills, which will help build your confidence.

CHAPTER TWO
How to Fit Your Putter

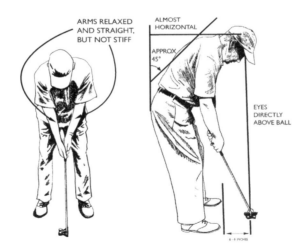

SUMMARY
Fit the putter such that your posture is comfortable, well balanced and the ball is directly below the eyes. Then make sure your arms are relaxed and relatively straight. In most cases putters are too long for golfers and don't allow them to make a natural swing because of too much tension in the arms which, in most cases, are bent to accommodate the putter which is too long.

CHAPTER THREE
The Grip

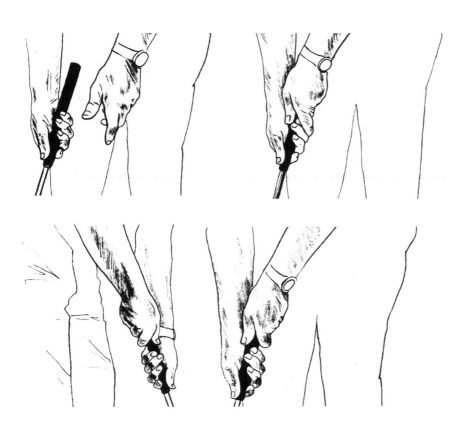

**TOP
ILLUSTRATION:**
First place
your right hand
on the grip
(*left*), then add
your left hand
as shown at
right.

**BOTTOM
ILLUSTRATION:**
For a right-
handed player,
left hand-low
grip (*left il-
lustration*); for
a right-handed
player, right
hand-low grip
(*right*).

SUMMARY

Have a comfortable but light grip and don't let your hands fight
each other. Select a method to hold the putter that best suits
you, then cut your putter to the correct length. This will help
remove doubt and allow you to focus on building your stroke.
Remember that a light grip is essential for good rhythm, which
in turn helps distance control.

CHAPTER FOUR
Ball Position

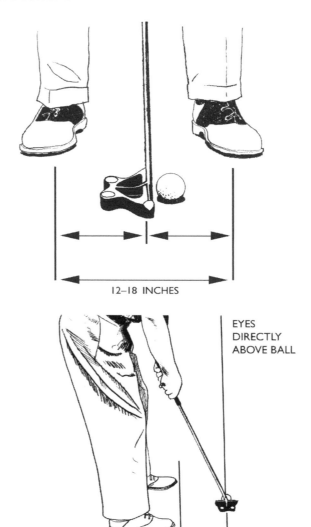

12–18 INCHES

EYES
DIRECTLY
ABOVE BALL

↗
The putter face should be positioned in the center of the stance.

6–8 INCHES

SUMMARY

The ball position should be between the feet — toes about 12 to 18 inches apart — about half the ball diameter forward of the centerline, but directly below the eyes. The feet are lined up parallel to the target line and the putter face should be on the centerline between the feet.

CHAPTER FIVE
Alignment & Why

Ideally, all of
your body
lines should be
parallel.

SUMMARY
Make sure that you avoid conflicting body parts by
aligning all body segments, feet, hips and shoulders
parallel to the ball/target-line plane.

CHAPTER SIX
Lock the System & Rock It

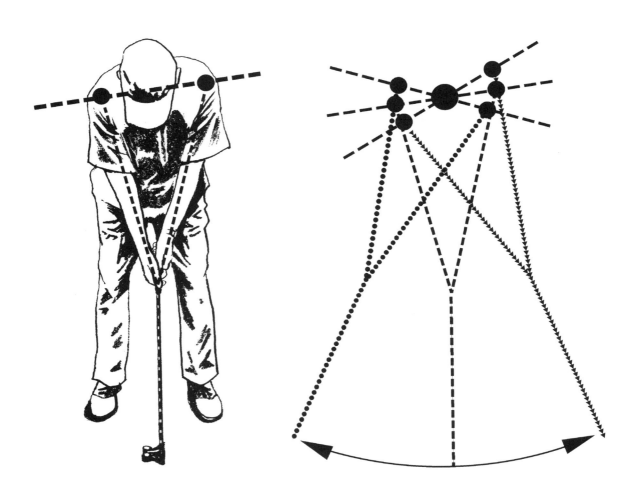

Lock and rock the system.

SUMMARY
Make sure we fix the system — shoulders, arms, wrists, hands and the putter — in place and rock it about the spine axis. This Lock and Rock fundamental will minimize the sources of error by restraining three DoF and thus minimize the sources of error associated with each.

CHAPTER SEVEN
The Secret: "Swing Plane of the Putting Stroke"

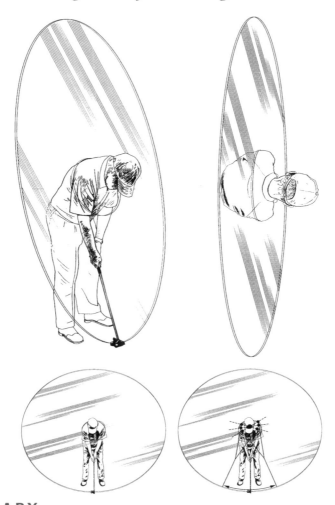

TOP ROW ILLUSTRATIONS: (*left*) The swing plane is inclined at about 10 degrees; (*right*). the swing plane as seen from above, describing a slight arc.

BOTTOM ROW ILLUSTRATIONS: The swing plane looking straight on at the golfer, incorporating the Lock and Rock.

SUMMARY

Once you fix the system creating a single unit — with as little tension as possible to maintain the system in place and our eyes over the ball — then you must swing this system in a plane inclined at about 10 degrees to the vertical. Do not rotate or break the wrists. The putter head, when swinging in the plane, will describe an arc when projected on to the ground, and will open and close before and after the impact relative to the ball. Nothing changes within the plane.

CHAPTER EIGHT
Find Your Natural Rhythm

➡️
**One-handed
putting is
excellent
practice to
help you
find your
rhythm.**

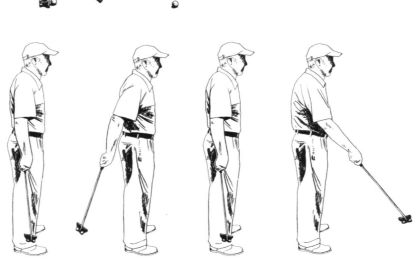

➡️
**Swinging
the putter
at your side
also helps
you find
your natural
rhythm.**

SUMMARY

**You have a natural rhythm based on the pendulum (single
unit) you have created — shoulders, arms, wrists, hands and
putter — and to find this rhythm practice putting with one
hand with a straight arm, fixed wrist and a very light grip.
Don't fight your natural rhythm, and make sure you have
the same rhythm for every putt.**

CHAPTER NINE
What Should You Be Looking at, Why & When?

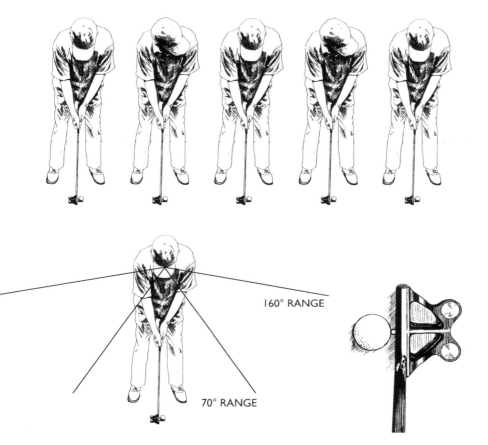

160° RANGE

70° RANGE

Take a couple of looks to connect to the hole.

Controlling our peripheral vision (*left*) is important when putting.

Keep your eye on a spot behind the ball.

SUMMARY

Imagine the shot during the pre-shot routine, then address the ball. Now aim the putter head at the Target Point along the target line. Connect to the hole by looking at a point — within approximately 12 inches of the hole — over which the ball will travel on its way into the hole. Look at this point and back to the ball a couple of times until you feel connected. Now, focus your eyes on a spot between the back of the ball and the clubface before, during and, for several seconds or more, after impact.

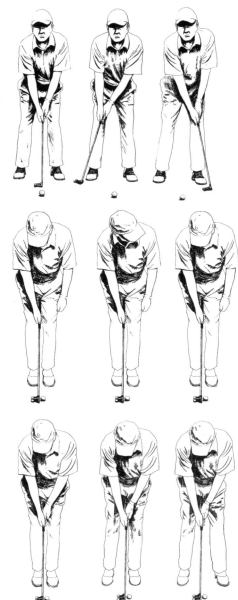

CHAPTER TEN
Planning & Pre-Shot Routine

Look at the hole while finding your rhythm and feel.

Be sure to aim the putter head carefully.

Take your stance.

SUMMARY

Analyze the situation and develop a solution to the challenge that you face on the green. Then prepare to implement your solution. This preparation should be very similar each time. Create an image of what you expect to happen and develop a feel (rhythm) for the stroke, bringing together the image and feel. Now, position yourself over the ball, aim the putter head at your target point, connect and finally focus your eyes on the contact point between the putter and the ball for several seconds after impact.

CHAPTER ELEVEN
The Fundamentals of Green Reading

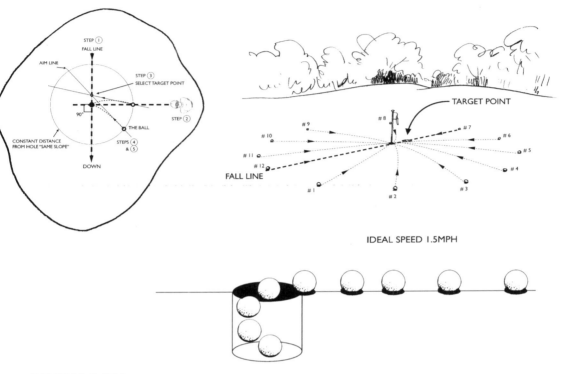

IDEAL SPEED 1.5MPH

SUMMARY

Find the Fall Line, estimate the break from a similar-length putt but at right angles to the Fall Line, select a Target Point and aim along this target line as if it was a straight putt. Remember that your putt should travel at a sufficient pace so it will hit the back wall of the cup. Don't expect to make every putt but believe you can.

I hope that you will now have a reasonably good understanding of WHAT you have to do to become a better putter and WHY. The putting stroke is a natural stroke and we have to recognize that as long as we apply the fundamentals the stroke is simple and intuitive. We must try to train the mind to guide, not interfere, and this is best done by developing confidence in our natural ability and Let it Happen.

ILLUSTRA-TIONS (*clock-wise, from top left*): **Step-by-step procedure for green reading; understand the Fall Line and the Target Point; speed of putt.**

13

HOW TO
PRACTICE
WITH
A PURPOSE

I F YOU ARE SERIOUS about improving your putting, you need to practice with a purpose — otherwise YOU ARE JUST WASTING YOUR TIME. ¶ Don't practice when you don't want to practice. You need to be motivated to improve and feel enthusiastic about what you must do to get better. ¶ You need positive feedback from practice sessions. Once you achieve your goal, STOP practicing. Leave the practice green feeling confident and positive. ¶ Practicing with a purpose might mean perfecting your mechanics, working on distance control or green reading, or all of the above. For example, work on your mechanics by hitting 20 or more balls at the hole from the same distance on a straight putt.

Make sure that:
- The ball position is correct;
- The alignment is correct;
- The shoulders, arms and wrists remain a stable, single unit;
- The putter head stays in plane;
- The eyes remain focused on a specific spot behind the ball from the take-away to well after impact and;
- Most importantly, that your rhythm remains constant.

We advise you to keep this book handy during the mechanics correction practice, especially Chapter 12 — the Quick Reference Summary chapter.

Once your mechanics match our prescription, then you must understand how to practice with a purpose by simulating what you would do on the course.

Just before teeing off, warm up on the practice green with two objectives — a) determine the green speed and calibrate yourself, and b) transfer your skills to the course by using only one ball and playing nine or so holes on the practice green. Make sure to complete each hole by sinking the putt. This sound builds confidence. Try not to repeat any putt.

This drill helps transfer good habits to the course. Make sure you follow your full pre-shot routine on every putt exactly the same way you play.

As in the case of Ivan Pavlov's dog, I am sure that a chimpanzee could sink a number of putts from eight feet if a bite of a banana was the reward and the chimp continued to hit putt after putt from the same distance. We call this the Chimp & Banana (C&B) practice drill.

Unfortunately, too many young golfers and others participate in the C&B drill, believing that this will make them better putters, while listening to tunes on their iPod, with their buds inserted — seemingly a permanent fixture — in their ears. This blocks out any auditory or meaningful feedback that they should be attending to.

Only hit many balls, one after the other from the same location, when working on the mechanics of your stroke. Once you have adopted the change then you need to work on implementing it by simulating what you will be presented with on the course OR developing confidence in this new move with specific and productive practice drills. The C&B is not one of them.

You need to do a little self-diagnosis and be perfectly honest with yourself. We must mentally list the putts we like and those we don't like – those we find difficult.

Here is a list of putts that you can rate on a scale of 1 (don't enjoy) to 10 (do enjoy). This is a start and only you know the truth about the ones you enjoy and the ones you don't.

We have listed the lengths as short (under 3 feet), mid (3-10 feet) and long (over 10 feet). You get the general idea, and can adjust the lengths as you see fit and/or add any other specific putts to this list that you feel need to be detailed:

Short, straight, uphill _____
Short, straight, downhill _____
Mid, straight, uphill _____
Mid, straight, downhill _____
Long, straight, uphill _____
Long, straight, downhill _____
Short, right to left, uphill _____
Short, right to left, downhill _____
Short, left to right uphill _____
Short, left to right, downhill _____
Mid, right to left, uphill _____
Mid, right to left, downhill _____
Mid, left to right, uphill _____
Mid, left to right, downhill _____
Long, right to left, uphill _____

Long, right to left, downhill _____
Long, left to right, uphill _____
Long, left to right, downhill _____

Upon completing this exercise, you will probably see a pattern in your responses. Is it the downhill putts that you don't like? Or the left to rights? Or the short putts?

Look at your responses, think about how the description of each made you feel and then you will have a better idea of what putts you need to confront because when you are playing on the course, you can't select only the putts you like.

In time, come back to this list and re-assess yourself. That way, you can gauge your improvement and stay on top of those putts that may be presenting a problem.

We tend to get pleasure by doing things we do well and avoid those we don't. Too often, we will hit the club we like best or hit our favorite shots over and over again, and why not, as this makes us feel good. However, we avoid practicing the hard-to-perfect shots that we don't do well or we find difficult, such as the downhill left-to-right slider.

What we need to do is learn how to overcome the fear of some difficult shots by coming to terms with the fact that they are difficult and we are not going to make many of them. We can choose to believe that we can make them, and develop confidence in knowing that we planned the shot correctly and executed it as well as we could. If we do this, we will avoid trying to manipulate the putt and wishing it into the hole — which results in fewer holed putts than a well-executed, confident stroke.

With the above in mind and having defined our strong and weak points, we must practice to develop confidence in all of our putts. Remember to practice your pre-shot routine on every practice putt. Every time you stroke the ball make sure you are doing it with the purpose of sinking the putt.

Don't let a bad pre-shot routine affect the putt — be it a

practice putt or one for real. If you are not properly prepared then don't expect a successful outcome.

Jack Nicklaus, whose preparation is legendary, offers some advice based on his own experiences:

"One of the most important things with me when putting is to make sure my lines are proper," says the Golden Bear. "By that, I want to make certain my eyes are on the line of the putter. If you drop the ball from your eyes, it would be on the line of where you're putting — I would keep my eyes on that or inside it.

"My tendency was that I would get outside over it," Nicklaus adds. "Since I was dominant left eye, I tried to putt so I would be more right-eyed, because I felt like I could see better down the line with my right eye. I worked on grip pressure all my life, and as far as the shaft of the putter, I made sure my hands were always equal to or in front of the ball. And I always felt like distance was more important than direction."

There are a number of drills we recommend that each serve a specific purpose but can be used to fine-tune your stroke, green reading, distance control and, most of all, confidence and how you execute the putt after you have planned it the best way possible.

PRACTICE DRILL NO. 1 — GREEN READING

P LACE SIX BALLS about 10 feet away from the hole, on the lower side if there is an obvious slope of approximately two or three percent (about 2 ½- to 3 ½-inch drop in a 10-foot putt).

Then walk around the hole to determine which ball will not break up the slope, i.e. which one is on the Fall Line. Place a coin behind this ball and then putt each ball at the hole for the sole purpose of determining if your choice of the

Fall Line was correct, i.e. did the ball in front of your coin not break.

You may have to do this a number of times on different holes until you start getting better at finding the Fall Line. Remember, if the area around the hole is "Planar" — i.e. this area within, say, the 10-foot radius all with the same slope – then each ball from the same distance within this area will have the same Target Point.

Every ball will break toward the Fall Line, so if your estimate of the Fall Line was correct then your only problem is to work out how much break to play.

When doing this you need to rely on your acquired abilities based on experience, but when you get better at determining the location of the Fall Line — this gets easier the more you do it — then move to a spot at 90 degrees to this Fall Line. This is where the break will be greatest and easier to estimate than from any other angle — except on the Fall Line itself.

Now assume a ball is situated at the 90-degree angle to the Fall Line but the same distance as your ball is from the hole. Select a Target Point above the hole on the Fall Line.

The Target Point for your ball is the same, no matter where it is, assuming the same distance from the hole and assuming the same slope (planar surface). This is an ideal situation that rarely exists but gives you a very good guideline as to what to expect.

This drill will do several things for you, such as finding the Fall Line more easily, providing a better estimate of the break and building your confidence in knowing that you have done your best in planning your pre-shot routine and going into auto-pilot mode to sink your putt.

We suggest positioning about eight balls in a circle equidistant from the hole on the practice green separated by an angle of 45 degrees and go through the procedure above and try to sink every putt.

With your same pre-shot routine, aim each putt at the Target Point and stroke it with enough pace that it hits the back of the cup — not dies in the hole. Don't repeat a putt that misses but continue around the compass. When you can sink every putt from four feet then move farther out.

During this practice drill, you will start recognizing how good your intuitive senses are, just like throwing a ball to someone without thinking, but just knowing how hard and which direction to throw it.

You must never underestimate your feel for the break. This is something we have developed and we have to trust ourselves. It does take a little practice and this drill will help.

PRACTICE DRILL NO. 2 — CONFIDENCE BUILDER

DO NOT EXPECT to sink every putt — but BELIEVE you can. This is our choice. A very good drill — which we frequently recommend to our elite and tour players to build confidence and have faith in their stroke through the knee-knocking zone — is detailed below.

This drill gets us through the no-confidence/no-faith zone and works well for all skill levels. Once we understand and can apply the fundamental mechanics then this drill becomes more subconscious without mental interference.

The high-confidence/low-stress zone is in the one- to two-foot range — IF we keep our eyes looking at the spot behind the ball during and after the stroke, and avoid "peeking."

There is little to no pressure on this short putt — except on the 18th to win a major — and, as a result, we can, and do, allow the body to do its thing. We have minimum stress and we "Let it Happen" — and generally sink the putt.

We start losing confidence and increase our stress level as the distance increases to the four-, eight- and 10-foot range, which is the low-confidence/high-stress zone. This is the "I hope it goes in" or the "P&P" (Putt and Pray) distance, where we try to wish the ball into the hole. We do this, especially on putts where we try to manipulate the putter head on the forward stroke, to follow the path we believe the ball is going to break, as if we had a guidance system attached to the ball.

This is the self-induced high-pressure zone, based on our own expectations and/or what we believe others expect of us. We question our own ability and lose faith in performing the act. So we look up, lose rhythm, punch the ball and steer the putter head — all leading to a manipulated stroke and, generally, a missed putt.

As the distance of the putt increases into the 15-foot zone and beyond, we start regaining our confidence in the stroke and have a relaxed, lower-stress putt and our mechanics improve.

We have more of a "Just-getting-it-close-will-do" attitude and, as a result, we can allow our abilities to play their part and, if things go right, we may even sink it. The pressure is relieved and we are through the pressure-manipulation zone.

The Drill:

T HE PROBLEM IS we know we can sink a one-foot putt, are reasonably sure we can sink a two-foot putt and if we focus we can sink a three-foot putt. However, we start to shake a little on four to 10 footers.

1. FIND THE FALL LINE — the no-break line — position a ball two feet from the hole along the Fall Line. Go through your full pre-shot routine and sink the putt with the ball hitting the back wall of the cup.

Remember to aim at a spot — a blade of grass — on the back rim of the cup, NOT AT THE HOLE itself.

Aiming at the HOLE, as a whole, from two feet is like aiming at a 50-yard wide fairway on your drive rather than a Target Point in line with where you would like the ball to end up.

Now select a Target Point and sink the two-foot putt with complete confidence. If you can do this with authority, then move to four feet, apply the same confidence and make the putt. Continue to move the ball away from the hole along the Fall Line in two-foot increments until you reach the 14-foot range.

Don't repeat a putt — except the first two-footer to develop the mindset of complete and utter confidence.

It is this mindset we must carry with us through all the putts to the 14-footer and farther.

Because you have convinced yourself that you are not going to sink every putt but believe you can, your expectations don't influence your physical performance.

Once you have successfully broken this mental barrier up the Fall Line, repeat the drill across the Fall Line. This repetition moving the ball back, two feet at a time while maintaining the same confident attitude that you can sink every putt, will help you perform more confidently and you will become a better putter.

PRACTICE DRILL NO. 3 — DISTANCE CONTROL

DISTANCE CONTROL is a matter of allowing natural intuition to work for you rather than trying to calculate how hard to hit the ball, how far to take the putter back or using paced measurements, charts or contour maps of greens.

Actually, we should not think about hitting the ball harder or softer but rather instinctively increasing or decreasing the length of the backstroke. This will — with consistent and good rhythm — increase or decrease the head speed and get more or less distance out of the putt.

How do we do this, and how can we practice doing this?

The answer to how we do this is the same as the answer

Sink putts from various distances with complete confidence.

to how fast do you have to move your hand to throw a ball to a person five feet away or 20 feet away?

Mother Nature, through our upbringing, gave us an innate ability to throw spears and darts at different targets, or balls to different bases, or make different-length putts without a connection to the Internet, or even a special App for your phone. We should rely on what nature gave us.

To bring this ability to the fore and thus respect what we have, we do need a little practice and the following drill will certainly help.

Situate yourself on a quiet practice putting green with about six to 10 holes cut in the green such that the holes are of varying distances from you. Take out a number of balls and putt one ball to each hole. Repeat this exercise several times.

Follow this drill with a putt to a short hole about five feet away, immediately followed by one to a long hole about 30 feet away. Do this about five times to the same two holes.

This exercise will show you how good you are at reading different distances by allowing your mind to process your visual observations and tell your body what to do.

Obviously putts which are downhill, uphill or sidehill, or all of the above, will challenge you and make the processing of all the information a little more complex, so you need to practice these using the suggested drill.

Trying to control distance by hitting balls to the edge of a green may help but this starts getting into the C&B (Chimp & Banana) practice-drill category. Again, hitting the ball to a single target over and over again is a waste of good practice time.

PRACTICE DRILL NO. 4 — FINDING YOUR RHYTHM

O
NE OF THE VERY BEST putting drills, especially to
find your rhythm, is to putt one handed. You can use
either hand, but we recommend the right hand if
you are right-handed.

Grip your putter with your right hand in a similar position and the same way you would grip the putter with this
hand. Address the ball as you would to make a two-handed
putt and place the left hand behind your back.

Now, with a straight but relaxed arm and a very light grip
— WITHOUT breaking your wrist or bending your elbow —
putt several balls at a hole about 10 feet away. You must allow
the putter to do all the work for you. Don't try to manipulate
the putter head or steer it in any way whatsoever.

Practice rhythm with one hand.

If you allow your natural ability to take over, the putter head will not move out of plane, i.e. it will open and close relative to the ground but will not change its orientation within the plane and will swing in a natural arc. Your wrists will not rotate.

The secret to one-handed putting is to use a very light grip. As soon as you are hitting the ball correctly you will know it, as the club will be doing all the work and each impact will feel SWEET. Few things feel better than a sweet one-handed putt.

Do this drill using 20 or more balls (this is not a C&B drill but a rhythm-building drill). Once you have developed confidence in the one-handed putts – this does not take long and you will certainly know it when you have arrived – then GENTLY place the other hand on the putter and continue to putt as if you were putting one handed.

There will be a little different motion as you place the other hand on the putter because you are now including your other arm and shoulders as part of the single unit. When you place both hands on the putter, the shoulders and arms are all added mass. The rhythm will be a little slower, but very similar.

You can use a one-handed swing in your pre-shot routine to get the feel and rhythm you will use in executing your plan.

PRACTICE DRILL NO. 5 — ONE BALL

BEFORE YOU GO OUT TO PLAY on the course, warm up by using one ball only on the practice green. If you do this you will be simulating what you do on the course while at the same time calibrating yourself to the speed of the greens for that day.

Make sure you go through your pre-shot routine for every putt on the practice green.

ALTERNATIVE

PUTTING STYLES

&

THE YIPS

T HIS SECTION — which covers alternative putting styles and putters to match — fulfills our need to provide comprehensive information, but does not imply that we suggest or recommend using these putting styles. In most cases we would only recommend one of these putting styles if the golfer has a back problem or another medical aliment that inhibits putting with a conventional putter and putting style. The other reason for using one of these alternative putting styles is if the golfer has the YIPS.

We have, in many cases, been able to cure the yips. However, this takes time and dedication by us and the golfer interested in solving his/her Yip problem. Using the Long putter has certainly helped golfers stay in the game and continue to enjoy playing long after they would otherwise give up golf.

We do not believe, and there is no sound evidence to show, that using one of the alternative styles of putting — i.e. Belly Putting, Long Putting, Side Saddle or PAL (Putter Arm Lock) — gives golfers an advantage over the conventional style of putting performed correctly in accordance with the Fundamentals of Putting.

Golfers with putting problems may choose an alternative (non-conventional) putting style, but in no case will this transform a good putter into a great putter. It may, however, turn a bad putter into a better putter.

14-1 PUTTING STYLES AND PUTTERS TO MATCH

PUTTERS ARE DESIGNED to make the process of putting efficient, comfortable and conforming with the Rules and traditions of Golf.

Given the size and shape of many of the putters designed within the last decade, the traditional part of this equation seems to have left the barn.

Many of the rules have been adapted to make it awkward to use a putting style which is not considered "traditional" in nature or which might give someone an undue assist and advantage in making a stroke. This could reduce the challenge the game presents and which makes it so attractive.

Two examples of non-traditional (and thus non-conforming to the Rules) approach to putting are a shuffle-board style of pushing the ball and a croquet style of putting with feet on either side of the intended line of the putt. So, as long as those styles of putting are not adopted, all that is required is that you strike the ball with the head of the club — any part of the head. Putter design makes it awkward and inefficient to hit the ball on any part of the head other than the face.

You can hold the putter any way you wish. You don't have to hold it on the grip. Your hands don't have to touch each other and you don't even have to use both hands to hold the putter.

The USGA & R&A are concerned about anchoring the putter to the body — presumably because it is non-traditional. There is no evidence to show the belly putter will turn a good putter — the golfer, not the instrument — into a great putter. It may turn a bad putter into a better putter but this is not enough to justify a change in the Rules regarding anchoring, which itself is hard to define.

Some good golfers have had relative success with Long putters and Belly putters but this is more out of necessity than gaining any significant advantage. The upside is that it has, in many cases, allowed golfers who would otherwise stop playing golf to remain in the game.

14-2 STANDARD-LENGTH PUTTERS

STANDARD-LENGTH PUTTERS vary in length from 30 inches to 35 inches for men and 28 inches to 34 inches for women. These lengths are within the standard range for a conventional style of putting. There is no need for putters to be swing weighted, which we will discuss, but changing a putter's length will affect the MOI of the club but have little effect on performance.

14-3 LONG PUTTERS

L ONG PUTTERS, in general, are for people who have specific problems with their putting. They are held with a split grip, holding the upper hand on the end of the grip and the hand against the body, anywhere from the lower chest to the chin. The club is anywhere from 46 to 50 inches long, the posture is generally upright and the putting plane shifts from the standard conventional putting style of about 10 degrees from vertical to about five degrees.

By holding the upper hand against the chest, the lower hand holds the putter at about 20 to 25 inches down the shaft from the grip end. There are generally two grips on the putter — permissible with putters only if both are round and do not have flat sides — or one very long grip, in which case a flat side is permitted.

14-4 HOW TO USE A LONG PUTTER

T HERE ARE TWO BASIC METHODS when using a Long putter: (A) Using the big muscles and keeping the shoulders, hands, arms and putter fixed as a single unit, the player pivots about the spine axis just below the neck or, if bent over, between the shoulders.

(B) Holding the shoulders still and keeping the butt end of the putter pinned to his/her chest, the player moves only the right hand and arm to swing the putter like a pendulum (tilted in a plane at about five degrees from vertical) suspended from the chest, pivoting the putter about the upper hand.

Method (A) is the preferred method because it does not require the right arm and hand to move independently of the shoulders as with method (B), which requires movement across the body using the arm to swing independently of the rest of the body.

When the arm (right arm and hand for a right-handed golfer) moves independently of the body, it is more difficult to keep the putter path in a plane on both the back and forward stroke. For this reason, Method (A) has proven to yield results that are more consistent.

The long putter style minimizes, if not eliminates, many body movements (DoF) that carry with them sources of error leading to inconsistent performance. For instance, using the previous discussion of DoF, we can see that the long putter practically eliminates three DoF — (1) moving the putter head Up and Down, (2) Opening and Closing the face by rotating the wrists and (3) Breaking the wrists.

Having said this, many have found that the use of the long putter on longer putts — where natural acquired ability plays a significant role — is a little more difficult and less consistent. It is similar to learning to walk with a splint on your leg. Eventually you may get to be very efficient at this, but it is obvious that you are somewhat handicapped.

14-5 BELLY PUTTERS

THE BELLY PUTTER is longer than the traditional putter — 40 to 45 inches long — but shorter than the Long putters, and has a conventional lie angle of 72 degrees. The reason for using a Belly, or Mid-length, putter is, in most cases, the same as those for using a Long putter –an inability to control a conventional-length putter or the tendency to break the wrists.

The advantage of using a Belly putter is that it takes the wrist break out of the stroke. The problem is that we introduce an additional problem in that the putter is pivoting about the belly — which should remain relatively static during the putting stroke — and the hands are pivoting about the shoulders.

This two-lever Belly putting system with two different pivot points is not noticeably awkward for small back strokes for short putts, but when you try to take the putter back for longer putts, it becomes more obvious that the right elbow must bend and the wrist breaks down to accommodate the motion. This breaking up of the single unit – as used in the conventional style of putting — adds a source of error rather than eliminating it as in the Long-putter style.

Alternate Style: Putter Arm Lock (PAL)
Using a Belly length putter against the left arm

THIS STYLE is more efficient than the Belly putter. When using a mid-length putter, the right-handed player extends the left arm fully, placing the left hand on the grip. The upper portion (above the left hand) of the putter grip rests against the left arm and the right hand is positioned on the end of the grip in the conventional manner, i.e. right thumb down. This upper hand then rests on the inner bicep portion of the left arm.

This grip minimizes the Up and Down DoF (Degree of Freedom) and eliminates the Wrist Break DoF while still maintaining a conventional stroke. This PAL style of putting would be a more efficient stroke than what is normally used with the Belly putter.

14-6 SIDE-SADDLE (SS) PUTTERS

WHEN SAM SNEAD was barred from using the croquet style of putting between his legs, he very successfully began to use a similar style still facing the hole. Sam used a standard-length putter and bent over, with both feet facing the hole while looking at the hole face-on with his head upright. He then tilted his head down with his eyes looking at the ball but off to one side with both feet on the same side of the line of the putt. The putter passing alongside his body, with the right hand low on the shaft with the left hand — thumb upward — on the top of the grip. This style became known as the Side-Saddle style of putting.

Two different methods of Side-Saddle (SS) putting have developed:

Side-Saddle SS (A):

FACING THE TARGET LINE and holding a Belly length putter — about 43 inches in length and a 72-degree lie angle — with a split grip. The right hand is low with the left hand holding the end of the grip with the thumb pointing upward, positioned directly in front of the middle of the chest with the left elbow anchored against the side of the chest. This is an upright version of the Sam Snead style.

Both feet are positioned facing the hole but with the right foot — for right-handed players — placed several inches behind the left foot. This right-foot position moves the right leg back to prevent interference of the right leg with the right forearm and hand when making the backstroke.

The pivot point is the left hand, and the right hand and arm form a single unit, with no option to break the wrist. This results in a natural (forward to aft) swinging motion, as in swinging the arm while walking.

Side-Saddle SS (B):

WITH STYLE SS (B) you are facing the target line, holding a long putter — about 44 to 48 inches in length and a 79-degree lie angle — with a split grip, right hand low and left hand at the end of the grip with the thumb pointing upward. The left hand is positioned close to the right armpit.

Position your feet with both facing the hole and the right foot slightly ahead of the left foot. This is optional as there is no interference with the swing, but finding good balance and a comfortable foot setup is important.

This style SS (B) allows the golfer to swing in a more up-right plane, i.e. at 85 to 90 degrees to the vertical as opposed to the 80-degree plane for conventional putting.

Both methods of the side-saddle (A) and (B) style will restrain or remove three DoF — the Wrist Break, the Up and Down, and the Opening and Closing of the face caused by rotation of the wrists.

14-7 ADVANTAGES OF SIDE-SADDLE (SS) PUTTING

THE ADVANTAGES ARE: 1) You are looking at the hole the same way you see life every day, with your head upright seeing the putt the way you normally look at things.

2) It is a more natural swing (not across the body but back and forth), like you are walking swinging your arms. This swing is also a little easier to stay in plane than an across-the-body swing.

3) You have reduced many sources of error.

4) If you have the yips it is a good way to find a way around this problem.

The disadvantages are:

1) With the first method SS (A) you are restricted in the movement by the body — your right leg.

2) In both methods (A) and (B) you lose some feel because you have restricted the DoF.

3) You may also find it a little more difficult to align the putter head.

4) You will need to practice it for a while before you develop confidence using it.

All of these disadvantages can be overcome very easily with practice. If you decide to switch to SS putting be prepared to practice using all the practice drills in Chapter 13.

UNDERSTANDING

YOUR

PUTTER

N O MATTER YOUR putting style or your preferred type of putter (discussed in Chapter 14), it certainly helps to know your putter and its technology designed to help you hole more putts.

15-1 KNOWING YOUR PUTTER

H OW MANY OF US have stored putters in closets, attics, garages, clubhouse lockers or elsewhere out of sight of our spouses and/or partners?

It has been said that to teach your naughty putter a lesson, leave it in a dark closet for several weeks and next time you let it see a putting green it will behave itself. Some putters are tied to the back of cars, dragged home and sometimes thrown in the lake for misbehaving.

Isn't it a shame that an inanimate object – as much as we have loved, accepted and hated it sequentially – can be the object of so much blame for our misapplication or misfortune?

When our putting goes wrong we look for the quick fix and too often this is to buy another one. For instance, $150 to $200 – the cost of a well-designed putter or, in some cases, a badly designed one — can buy us a good lesson or two from a qualified Certified Putting Instructor (CPI) who truly understands the fundamentals of putting.

Every serious race-car driver should know something about the car he/she is driving, as too should every serious golfer be better informed about the putter he/she is about to buy or is using.

In this section of our book we will explain the basic properties of a putter and what to look for when you next decide to buy one.

15-2 THE CLUB DEFINED

P UTTERS ARE GOLF CLUBS defined in the Rules of Golf for a specific use and, as such, have restrictions placed on them unlike those for irons and woods.

"Definition: A 'Putter' is a club with a loft not exceeding

10 degrees designed primarily for use on the putting green." (Appendix II 1a, Rules of Golf)

This does not mean you can't use it elsewhere, but it is specifically designed for putting.

Definition: The "Putting Green" is all ground of the hole being played that is specially prepared for putting or otherwise defined as such by the Committee. A ball is on the putting green when any part of it touches the putting green.

15-3 MATERIALS, STRUCTURE, IMPACT AND FEEL

B ECAUSE THE PUTT requires only low-speed impact, the putter can have design features — such as structural members, attachments, two grips and neck joints — that may not stand the impact forces experienced by an iron or a wood club, and whose purpose may be for feel or forgiveness purely aesthetic in design.

The feel we get from a putter is mainly the sound during impact, but it is also the vibration after impact. The vibration generally comes from flexible structural members and/ or off-center impact. For instance, even though the structural members of the putter, i.e. the attachments and/or cross members (in a multi-beamed, lattice-type mallet design) seem to be rigid but in many cases during impact these do give a little and thus affect the feel of a putt.

Inserts:

A NOTHER CONTRIBUTOR to the feel of a putter is the material it is made of, which in most cases is milled or cast steel. To soften the sensation and sound at impact, designers often place an insert in the face of the putter. In some cases, this insert is also designed to affect the spin rate on the ball.

At this point, it is important to note that the Rules do not permit any treatment to the face that will unduly influence the movement of the ball, including how much more or less spin it imparts when compared with a standard steel face.

Despite this admonition, some putter designers claim that their treatment to the face or insert does have a significant effect on the spin on the ball. And while claims of this nature form a large part of the marketing efforts for many putter companies, the only thing that seems to be certain is that inserts absorb some of the force and impact, resulting in the ball leaving the club face at a lower speed than with a club without an insert.

If an insert is not part of the putter's design, aluminum, brass or other soft metals are the materials of choice. In most cases these softer materials will have the benefit of producing a good sound (and thus feel) and it will not be necessary to have an insert.

Loft:

THE FACT IS that a well-designed putter should have about four degrees of loft in order to launch the ball out of its standing position depression on the green, thus making the ball launch predictably consistent. The ball leaves the ground slightly with very little backspin or some times no spin, and touches down, starts skidding and sliding. The distance it is airborne is dependent on the impact speed, but for a 10-foot putt this is about four inches.

The ball will start to have pure rolling rotation (spin) about 15 percent of total putting distance. A putter with no loft and moving horizontally into the impact zone will drive the ball into the side of the depression — which, by the nature of depressions, is inconsistent in depth — and hop out differently for each depression depth. A putter with a loft of two degrees or less will be inclined to do this.

Manufacturing technique:

THE MOST ACCURATE METHOD of making a putter is by machining it to the exact dimensions required. Robotic CNC (Computer Numerical Control) machines are used for this purpose, as they are for critical aircraft and spacecraft parts. The process starts with a block of the material used for the body of the putter, clamped in place. Based on the computer program, a robot selects tool bits, which are used to machine the shape of the putter head. This process reproduces the shapes dimensions to an accuracy of 0.001 of an inch, every time.

This final part will be polished and treated as required before prepared for assembly into a putter.

15-4 MOMENT OF INERTIA (MOI)

BECAUSE WE ARE NOT all capable of making contact with the ball at the exact center of percussion (sweet spot) of the face of a putter, it is important to design the putter in a manner to reduce the effect, both in direction and ball speed, of a mis-hit.

To do this most effectively, one needs to increase the moment of inertia of the putter. What is moment of inertia, or MOI?

MOI is the measure of the resistance to (angular acceleration) sudden twisting on impact. A simple way to demonstrate it is as follows. Take two 20-pound weights and hold each of them close to your chest. Now try to twist quickly back and forth around your spine. This should be relatively easy to do.

Now, extend your arms out sideways with the weights in your hands, keeping your arms and shoulders stiff. Now try to twist back and forth around your spine quickly. You will find it more difficult to do, because the weights are extended outward away from your spine.

What you have done is increase the MOI of the system (your

body with extended arms) about your spine (vertical) axis.

When we talk about MOI, generally the discussion involves iron and wood club design. However, a high MOI is probably as important and more desirable in putters than the other clubs.

For instance, if you make contact away from the center of the putter face, you want it to resist twisting about the axis that runs vertically through the head, during impact. To do this one needs to have a putter with the weight distributed to the heel and toe of the head, thus increasing the putter's MOI about the vertical axis.

The result is a larger area of forgiveness across the face. Today, this one attribute describes the toe-heel-weighted putter, a style created by the Ping Anser many years ago.

However, there is a second axis to consider, one that makes the putter forgiving up and down the face. To get this forgiveness, one must increase the MOI about an axis, which goes through the putter head from toe to heel. To do this one needs to increase the size of the head backward, and weight is added to the back section of the head as far away from the face as possible.

This would be a mallet-style putter, such as the Frankly Frog, with the center of gravity far back from the face. This allows for a high MOI about the vertical axis (forgiveness from toe to heel) and a high MOI about the toe/heel axis (behind the face) maximizing forgiveness up and down on the face.

The bonus in this case is the location of the center of gravity (c.g.) far behind the face and commonly accepted shaft location. This helps in achieving a face-balanced putter without additional joints or shaft bends.

The concept of splitting the rear weights helps maximize the MOI within an acceptable and aesthetically pleasing size as well as helps stabilize the putter feel by having a high MOI about the axis which goes through the face to the back of the putter.

The Frankly Frog Putter is one of the most stable, well-balanced and forgiving putting instruments available.

SPLIT TUNGSTEN
WEIGHTS

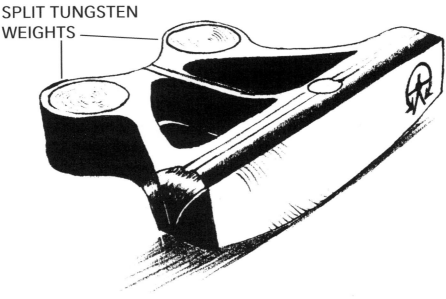

↗
**The split
tungsten
weights of
the Frankly
Frog increase
the MOI and
forgiveness
factor.**

15-5 CENTER OF GRAVITY (C.G.)

A S MENTIONED in the discussion about MOI, we need to move the center of gravity (c.g.) back and distribute the weight away from the c.g. to make it more forgiving. But as we will explain, we also need to keep the c.g. as low in the head as possible.

When the player places the putter behind the ball resting on the ground, the contact point with the center of the ball on the face is 0.84 inches above the sole. However, during a stroke, the putter head is raised above the green surface by up to 0.25 of an inch. Raising the club by this much will lower the impact point on its face to about 0.60 inches above the sole. If during the stroke the putter is raised more than 0.25 of an inch, then the contact point on the face is lowered even more.

Most blade-style putters have a c.g. location about 0.65 inches above the sole, which means that contact will be made with the ball on, or below, the c.g. of the head in normal putting conditions.

Because of the low toe/heel axis MOI – low forgiveness up and down the face — of the blade-style putters, the forgiveness of a mis-hit up and down the face is not very efficient in the transfer of momentum. The result of this kind of mis-hit is a real drop in distance for the same head speed. This type of stroke happens often when putting the ball resting against the fringe of the green or when we mis-hit it on the bottom section of the putter face.

A lower c.g., and one that is well back from the face, increases the forgiveness up and down as well as toward the toe to heel and thus will increase, so to speak, the size of the sweet spot. This results in a more efficient impact with the ball and thus more consistent distance control.

15-6 SOLE DESIGN

S OLE DESIGN is something that has been ignored in many of today's putters. The default design today for putter soles is relatively flat, especially in the larger mallet-style putters. A flat sole, however, can have a detrimental affect on the putting stroke in a number of ways, such as the setup is fixed when the putter is soled at address as designed, the undulations in the green will affect the lie angle at address and the putter toe or heel will likely scuff the green as it approaches the ball just before impact.

For instance, a small error in the swing plane and/or green undulation, combined with insufficient rise angle of the head during the swing, will result in the toe or heel of the putter contacting the green surface before impact. This will send the ball in a direction far off target.

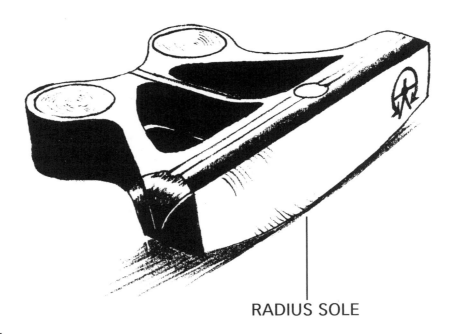

RADIUS SOLE

The Frankly
Frog has a
radius sole.

A radius from toe to heel on the sole, on the other hand, will allow for undulations and slight imperfections in posture and setup — i.e. a more forgiving sole as was the case with one of the most popular putters in the 1960s, Acushnet's Bulls Eye putter (a true blade putter).

Not having a flat sole from face to back creates its own challenges. If a mallet putter's sole is not flat from the face to a point slightly back of the point directly below the head's c.g., then the putter will not sit correctly at address. The result will be a tendency of the club's c.g. to create a slight force to twist the head off line at address when it is soled.

Players often say that a particular putter sits open or closed at address, even though it has a flat sole from face to back. This, in many cases, is the fault of the user. If the putter is sitting behind a ball that is correctly positioned between the feet, but the hand position is forward, then the face will open up. Obviously if the hands are behind the neutral position, the face will tend to close.

15-7 PUTTER LIE ANGLE

THE LIE ANGLE for a putter is not as important with regard to the direction off line of the ball (left to right) as it is for lofted clubs, such as wedges. This is because the loft on a putter is only four degrees. However, the lie angle is important when it comes to setup. One does not want the putter to be toe-up or heel-up at address.

As we have already covered in the second Fundamental of Putting, the suggested posture at address is slightly bent legs, feet about 12 to 18 inches apart (shoulder width is a good starting point) and a comfortable, relaxed forward bend. In this position when the player grips the CORRECT LENGTH PUTTER with arms hanging loose, relatively straight and vertically down with the clubhead directly below the eyes (about eight inches from the toes), the lie angle will be very close to 72 degrees for most golfers.

This may vary a couple of degrees, but on average this lie angle is best suited to almost every golfer using a conventional stroke. A different lie may be required for an unconventional style or for long putters, but this will only encourage the golfer to remain with a style of putting which will not produce a consistent stroke unless he/she works hard to perfect this style and minimize the sources of error.

15-8 PUTTER BALANCE AND WEIGHT

PUTTER BALANCE relates to "feel" when, in the address position, the player swings the club back and forth as if to make a stroke. Weighting, equally distributed toward the toe and heel of the putter head about the shaft axis, will make it feel properly balanced.

If, however, the shaft axis is close to the heel and away from the (center of gravity) c.g. when the putter is waved back and forth, it will tend to over rotate when there is a change of direction. This can contribute to a very slight sensation, which will affect the "feel" or balance of the putter.

Swing-weight balancing — often talked about when referring to putter balancing — is something we must avoid. The only time we need to discuss swing weight is for clubs other than putters. Swing weight is a trial-and-error derivative of System MOI (the resistance to angular acceleration when rotated about a defined axis) and is most important when balancing and matching clubs – different weights and different lengths — in a set, and only when a full swing is being used.

The most important weight in the putter is the head weight. This is the business end of the putter and we need to learn how best to swing it consistently.

After many years of trial and error, a putter head weight

of 350 grams seems to work best for 95 percent of all golfers.

Over time heavier and lighter putter weights have been tried, but we always migrate back to what works most efficiently and "feels" best.

Some people have suggested the player should change the weight of his/her putter for different green speeds. This is certainly not a good idea. Changing the putter's weight will change the overall feel, and the player will have to develop a new rhythm and feel for this change in weight. There are enough variables to worry about when putting, and introducing another one is not a smart thing to do.

15-9 THE PUTTER GRIP

THE GRIP OF A PUTTER comes in various sizes. In most cases the standard grip size works best for most golfers. A player can increase the size of the grip slightly by wrapping extra tape around the shaft before putting the grip on the putter, or the player can order larger grips if they feel that the need something bigger than a standard grip size.

Very large grips are inclined to prevent the wrists from rotating when used with irons and woods, but there is little evidence to show that they help in putting other than to help promote gripping the putter with less pressure. We recommend a light grip pressure to reduce tension in the arms, and sometimes a large grip may tend to do this and in turn maintain good rhythm.

A few touring professionals have had success with larger grips, but there is no magic in changing from a standard grip size unless the golfer has larger hands than normal and is uncomfortable with the standard size.

Most putter grips have a flat side for the purpose of positioning of the hands — generally the thumbs on the flat — consistently each time. The grips for the rest of the clubs in your set must be round, i.e. no flat sides, if they are to conform to the Rules of Golf.

15-10 PUTTER HEAD SHAPE

PUTTER HEADS come in various shapes, and just by looking at them, you can normally tell how the weight of the putter head is distributed and what that means for playability.

True Blade:

AN EXAMPLE of a true blade is a Cash-In or a Bulls Eye putter —the most popular putters in the 1950s and 1960s. These have relatively thin heads from face to back (about a half-inch) and are about 4¼ inches long. They generally have two faces and, if so, the lofts and other characteristics of each must be the same. The true blade style of putter has a low MOI (about the vertical axis) and is not forgiving on mis-hits.

Modern Blade:

A POPULAR SHAPE putter for many years has been the toe/heel-weighted putter such as the Ping Anser — copied many times with only slight variations. This putter has a higher MOI about the vertical axis than the true blade and is forgiving in mis-hits in the toe/heel direction. When struck on the lower leading edge, however, these putters lose a sweet impact feel and the ball speed is affected significantly which results in lack of distance control and often putts left short.

Mid Mallet:

THE MID-MALLET PUTTERS are relatively broad from face to back and have more weight distributed to the outer perimeter and a c.g. farther back than the toe/heel-weighted blades. The head weight of these mid-mallet putters is about the same as the toe/heel-weighted blades, between 330 and 380 grams.

True Mallet:

THE TRUE MALLET has a larger head, with the weight distributed as far as possible from the c.g., which is about 1.5 inches behind the face (halfway to the back of the head). The better mallets have extreme weight distribution while still being pleasing to the eye. In some cases, a heavy metal, such as tungsten (twice the density of lead and the same as gold) is used to maximize the balance and dynamic properties of the putter but maintain the good looks. A good example of this is the original Frankly Frog model.

From left to right, a True Mallet, a Mid-Mallet, a Modern Blade, a True Blade.

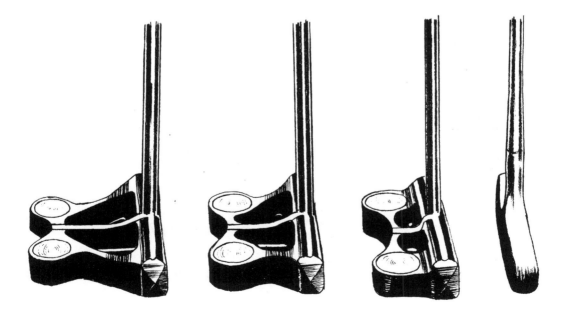

15-11 PUTTER FACE TREATMENT

THE RULES OF GOLF do not allow any treatment to the club face that will unduly influence the movement of the ball. This means that the putter face must in general be hard and rigid. Some exceptions, however, may be made for putters.

This is why we see inserts in putter faces to dampen the sound and lower the COR of the impact. In many cases the newer, harder balls will have a harsh sound off a steel putter face, so putter manufacturers have inserts to dampen the sound. Some manufacturers have created putter faces with grooves to do the same thing, and have claimed that this places topspin on the ball. These claims are worthy of challenge and may be contrary to what is permitted under the Rules.

In the past, some putter faces have had a mirror-like polished finish, because it was felt that a slight roughness in the putter face would deflect the ball. This is not true. In fact, there is a certain amount of roughness required to prevent the possibility of slippage on the face during impact.

15-12 SHAFT LOCATION

SINCE A PUTTER SHAFT is not designed to generate as much head speed as possible with the least amount of work, the putter shaft should be stiff and of average weight. There are stiff graphite shafts designed for wedges that also work for putters. They can be used to eliminate the reflection off steel and also allow for the contrasting color (i.e., white on black) for special aiming graphics.

Shafts are attached to various parts of the head but mainly to the heel or center, and are either straight or have an off-set goose-neck. The heel-shafted putter normally has a bend in the shaft to more closely align the main portion of the shaft

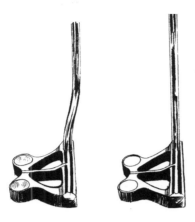

axis to be in line with the c.g. or directly in front of it toward
the target. This is known as a face-balanced putter.

A very popular configuration of heel-shafted, blade-type
putters is with an off-set. This is popular because the off-set
moves the shaft axis ahead of the face and away from the c.g.
and closer to face-balancing. This tends to better align the
face — not as much as true face balancing — at impact to be
closer to right angles to the putter head's path at impact.

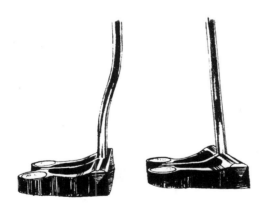

The off-set also positions the shaft slightly (from a half
to one full shaft diameter) ahead of the face. This will allow
the shaft to be vertical at address and the ball position to be
slightly farther back than with a center-shafted putter with
no off-set.

The change in ball position at address could be considered one of the most important factors as to why someone would choose an offset putter. The off-set design also provides a slightly better view of the face behind the shaft. Another reason a person may consider an off-set putter includes a preference due to visual perception and comfort level. However, it should be noted that these two factors are generally not important enough to have any measureable effect on putting performance.

15-13 RULES GOVERNING PUTTERS

"**A** PUTTER IS A CLUB *with a loft not exceeding 10 degrees designed primarily for use on the putting green.*"

— *2012-2015 Rules of Golf*

A putter is a utility club, and does not need to match or bear any relationship to the specifications of the rest of your set — such as swing-weight, overall weight, shaft flex, length, etc.

Because the rules are more lenient for a putter, allowing it to have certain features not otherwise afforded to iron and wood clubs, the limitations placed on it — i.e. loft of no more than 10 degrees and lie angle of not greater than 80 degrees — have been adopted to make it awkward to use efficiently in a non-traditional manner on the putting green.

While the putter is designed for use on the putting green, there is no rule in the book that requires you to use a specific club for any particular purpose. Thus, you can putt with any club in your bag, just as you can play a shot from anywhere on the golf course with a putter. It's just not advisable to do so.

That said, the Rules of Golf consider a putter to be a club, thus the same rules apply to putters as other clubs, with some exceptions:

- A putter, as with all clubs, must be traditional and customary in form and make.
- A putter must be plain in shape, but holes are allowed from the top to the bottom or elsewhere but not through the face.
- A putter must not be easily adjustable.
- The putter may not have a loft of more than 10 degrees.
- The putter shaft, as with other clubs, must diverge from the vertical by more than 10 degrees when in the normal address position.
- The shaft must not bend forward (toward the target line) more than 20 degrees or backward more than 10 degrees.
- There is no upper limitation on the length of a putter but it must be longer than 18 inches.
- The shaft can be fixed to any part on the head.
- The neck or socket can not be longer than five inches in length above the sole as measured along the axis of the bend.
- The grip may have flat sides but should not be molded for any part of the hands.
- A putter may have two grips, but if so they must be circular in cross section and separated by more than 1½ inches.
- The grip must extend to the end of the shaft.
- The axis of the grip need not coincide with the axis of the shaft.
- A putter may have two striking faces, but they must have the same characteristics and be opposite each other.
- The distance from the heel to the toe must not be greater than seven inches.
- The distance from the top of the head to the sole may not be more than 2½ inches.
- There is no limit on the COR for putters.
- The face must be hard and rigid and may have grooves, etc., without limitation except that these markings are

not designed to unduly influence the movement of the ball.

- The distance from heel to toe must be greater than the distance from face to back.
- The distance from the heel to the toe of the face must be greater than or equal to two-thirds of the distance from the face to the back of the head.

With the above in mind and used as a guide, if there is any doubt as to the conformity of a putter, it is strongly suggested that you contact the R&A or USGA to get some advice.

15-14 IMPACT BALL LAUNCH

WHEN THE BALL is struck by a putter it will generally leave the ground slightly because of the putter's loft — four degrees is preferable — and the upward direction of the head path. The ball will remain off the ground for about three to four percent of the overall distance of the putt. It then will slide or skid for another 10 to 11 percent of the distance of the putt. Thus the total distance that the ball goes before it takes on pure rolling spin is about 13 to 15 percent of its total distance.

For example, on a 10-foot putt you can expect the ball to be in flight for 3½ to 4½ inches and then it will start skidding and start a forward roll for 12 to 13 inches – a total of about 15 to 17 inches before taking on pure rolling. Thereafter the ball will be rolling with pure forward rolling spin and will be slowed down by rolling friction (dependent on green speed) and gravity, if it is uphill. A downhill putt will slow down less because gravity is helping it on its way. Gravity – in the form of slopes in the putting green – will also influence how much it breaks left or right. An uphill putt travels faster and for a shorter time than a downhill putt.

15-15 FACE ANGLE AT IMPACT

W E ARE OVERLY OBSESSED with face angle at address. This is important but not nearly as important as face angle at impact. Some good golfers may have a two-degree-open face at address, but it is perfectly perpendicular to the target line at impact. In most cases, however, a perfect address face angle is a fairly good indication that the face will get back to this position at impact.

The head path can be outside in (across the target line) by as much as four degrees — this applies initial sidespin — but this will influence the ball direction by less than one degree if the face is pointing at the target line during impact. So face angle is more important than head path.

But to be safe, try to get the head path to be traveling along the target line with the face angle 90 degrees (perpendicular) to the target line just before and during impact. The impact will be more efficient and the distance more consistent.

15-16 FACE LOFT AND HORIZONTAL HEAD PATH

Face Loft:

A S MENTIONED EARLIER, the loft of a putter may not be more than 10 degrees — otherwise it is not considered to be a putter and different design specifications apply. However, most good putters have a loft of about four degrees and as little as two degrees. Bobby Jones' putter (Calamity Jane) had eight degrees of loft, which was necessary to cope with the slow greens that confronted him.

A faster green will not require as much loft as a slow green, but for most competition green speeds of 11 to 13 feet on the Stimpmeter a four-degree loft works well, especially if there has been some significant traffic at the end of the day or competition.

Horizontal (Vertical Plane Arc) Head Path:

THE HEAD PATH during impact in the vertical plane will influence the launch angle of the ball but not by as much as the loft. In a previous discussion, we talked about the head path across the line of putt and indicated that the face angle influenced the direction of the putt from three to four times more than the head path across the ball.

Similarly, the loft angle of the putter at impact will influence the direction of the ball launch angle by three or four times more than the upward or downward direction of the head at impact.

15-17 FORWARD PRESS

MANY GOLFERS believe that a forward press will induce topspin. This is not true. A forward press, if held through impact, takes loft off the putter and will thus reduce the distance of lift off the green but not the amount of skidding and sliding before pure rolling.

What a forward press will do — if you hold the press throughout the stroke — is decrease the loft at impact. A reduced loft of more than two degrees (on a four-degree lofted putter) will tend to drive the ball into the side of the depression in which it is sitting and cause it to jump differently each time, depending on the size of the depression and the length of the grass. A ball will settle more on a slow green than a fast green.

A forward press — if not too severe — is often used as a trigger to start the stroke. Many times golfers have a problem in starting the stroke from a static position to a smooth takeaway and need a trigger to do so. But it must be made clear that a forward press is more beneficial mentally than mechanically.

Golfers do sometimes add or subtract loft by having the hands ahead of the putter head during impact. This is seldom because the arc is in a downward direction at impact but rather that the hands are leading the head. This takes on the same result as a forward press, but it has been set sometime during the back stroke or returning forward stroke.

CONCLUSION

THIS PUTTER TECHNOLOGY chapter is useful in the process of selecting a putter and will hopefully give you ammunition to fight off some of the myths surrounding putters.

THE LAST PUTTER YOU WILL NEED TO BUY: Once you have found a putter that is properly fitted, well designed and feels good, don't change it or tie it to the back of your car and drag it home. It is not the putter that is misbehaving — it is our inability to apply the fundamentals and allow our mind to "get out of its own way."

Just believe and
Let it Happen.

ACKNOWLEDGEMENTS

S PECIAL THANKS to all those who have supported our passion for helping golfers putt better over the years. You know who you are and we greatly appreciate your many words of encouragement, your actions and your belief in us.

In creating this book, a very special thanks goes to the following members of our Certified Putting Instructor (CPI) Advisory Board who reviewed our preliminary draft and offered excellent feedback and advice:

Dr. Bob Christina
Dr. Debbie Crews
Dr. Phil Martin
Dr. Joan Vickers

And the other researchers with whom we communicate frequently.

Also to Steve Donahue, our gifted editor and a freelance writer/editor whose 21-year golf-industry career has included managing editor/writing stints at Golf Digest and GOLF Magazine publications, covering golf equipment and travel.

And Grant Carruthers, our talented United Kingdom-based illustrator whose brilliant illustrations and diagrams so deftly brought The Fundamentals of Putting principles to life.

And last, but by no means least, Tim Oliver, our skilled book designer, who is an art director at *Golf Digest* and a freelance book designer, with previous art director stops at *Time Magazine,* the *New York Times* and *Detroit Free Press.*

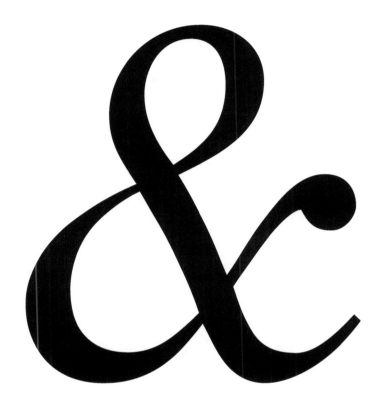

APPENDIX

NOTE FROM THE AUTHORS

Frank Thomas:

OUR INTERNATIONALLY recognized team of advisors is unsurpassed for their contributions to the game and their collective knowledge about the science of golf. They also have made significant contributions to our online Certified Putting Instructor (CPI) course, from which much of this book's contents have been garnered.

As mentioned before we have tried to keep the scientific nomenclature to a minimum and use more commonly used terms for a better understanding of the concepts presented. At the end of this Appendix we have referenced some reading materials for those who need a more in-depth understanding of the science

My passion for golf started at the age of eight. Throughout my career I have not only tried to inspire others to play and experience the game, but also to use whatever influence I have to help golf's administrators maintain the respect they deserve by effectively exhibiting their wisdom.

I know that this book will help every golfer interested in improving his/her performance and gaining confidence on the putting green.

Read, Learn, Apply, Practice and then
"Let it Happen"

Valerie Melvin:

MY PASSION for putting started on the practice putting green at Clydebank and District Golf Club in Scotland, where I spent most of my time while growing up and playing golf. I enjoyed not only the solitude of practice but also the competitive games with the other juniors.

As day became night and eventually the green was illuminated only by the clubhouse's light, I worked tirelessly on my putting, eventually representing Scotland in international matches. The putting green was central to my development as a golfer. Putting was a powerful part of my game, helping me win countless matches and shoot some great scores.

When you are putting well, there is a feeling, a confidence, a flow. It is almost magical — you can see the ball go in the hole even before stroking it.

When I studied psychology at Stirling University I conducted my research on brain activity prior to the golf putt. Understanding the mind's activity when putting was intriguing.

Over the last 12 years, Frank and I have been devoted to trying to understand even more and, more importantly, passing it onto other golfers and professionals so everyone can improve this crucial part of their game.

This book has been a culmination of many years of observation, experimentation and review. Working with Frank is an amazing experience. He has the most-brilliant mind and sees things in a unique way. It has been a privilege and an honor to accompany him on our journey to help others.

THE STIMPMETER

THE HISTORY OF the Stimpmeter — the universally recognized device used to measure the speed of greens — needs to be told. In 1976, while working for the USGA, Al Radko — director of the green section staff who was studying the effect of spike marks — asked me to develop a device to measure the speed of greens. He gave me a device he found, which was designed by Eddie Stimpson in 1935, and said it didn't work very well. It consisted of a molding-like wood section with a concaved, semicircular groove down one side. A ball was placed in an indentation in the groove about 12 inches from the tip end, which rested on the green's surface. When the device was lifted from the other end the ball released and rolled down the piece of wood onto the green.

To make this relatively crude device more consistent, I designed — on paper — several devices that would launch the ball at a consistent-enough speed for a minimum 10-foot roll on an average green with pure rolling spin once it contacted the green surface. These designs had leveling devices, triggers and other adjustable legs, etc.

I immediately recognized that these intricate and delicate designs would work well but were too cumbersome for every-day use. I abandoned my designs and revisited Eddie Stimpson's concept. I redesigned it to be more accurate and increase the roll to differentiate between speeds more effectively. Out of respect for Eddie's initial idea and concept, we called it the Stimpmeter.

With the help of a local cabinetmaker — Mr. Boehs in Chester, N.J. — we made five wooden prototypes and distributed them to green-section members, who measured hundreds of greens in 35 states across the United States. The data was analyzed and used to establish some initial standards and recommendations for green speeds.

The Stimpmeter is now used worldwide, and its measurements are referred to during every televised golf event.

At last we were able to quantify the speed of greens based on a standard launch condition — a ball releasing from a precisely machined slot when the device was inclined at a specific angle (close to 20 degrees). This takes advantage of one of Nature's universal constants — almost — i.e. the force of gravity which helps initiate the ball's release out of the slot to start its 30-inch roll down a runway before touching the green's surface.

The sizes of the ball and the precisely machined slot dictate when the ball releases from the slot while tilting the Stimpmeter slowly from one end, with the opposite end resting on the green.

If the Stimpmeter is tilted reasonably slowly, it produces very consistent results. There is a small bounce as the ball contacts the green, but the negligible effect doesn't detract from the device's ease of use and effectiveness.

Unfortunately (in the minds of some golfers) you are not permitted, under the Rules of Golf, to use a Stimpmeter during a tournament.

However, with the green superintendent's ability to maintain specific green speeds throughout the course and on the practice green, you can calibrate for green speed on the practice greens which, in most cases, is the same as on the course's putting surfaces so you aren't surprised when you reach the first green.

In the practice drills chapter we discuss a pre-round warm up using only one ball on the practice green, allowing you to simulate what you do on the course while simultaneously calibrating yourself to that day's green speed.

The science of how and why a golf ball follows a parabolic curve is interesting and helps curious golfers understand why, on a breaking putt, the ball (5.278 inches in circumference) dives left or right during its last rotation just before coming to rest. However, we have covered in the green reading chapter the must-know basics of reading greens without it becoming a physics lesson.

For those who insist on getting down to the nitty-gritty of the physics, we would like to refer you to the works of H.A. Templeton, in "Vector Putting," Frank Werner & Richard Grieg, in "Better Golf from New Research" and Robert Grober in "The Geometry of Putting On a Planar Surface."

— Frank Thomas

FURTHER READING SELECTIONS
Suggested reading for interest and the science of golf:

BOOKS
Alpenfels, E., Christina, B., and Heath C., *Instinct Putting,* Gotham Books, 2008

Templeton, H.A., *Vector Putting,* Vector Golf Inc., 1984

Vickers, J.N., *Perception, Cognition, and Decision Training: The Quiet Eye in Action,* Human Kinetics, 2007

Werner, F.D. and Greig, R.C., *Better Golf from New Research,* Origin Inc., 2001

SCIENTIFIC PAPERS
Some fascinating scientific papers related to putting can be found in the Science and Golf series, which are Proceedings of the World Scientific Congress of Golf. Find out more at *www.golfscience.org*

Grober, R.D., *The Geometry of Putting On a Planar Surface,* 2011

The full paper may be found at http://arxiv.org/ftp/arxiv/papers/1106/1106.1698.pdf
A You Tube video demonstrating this may be watched at http://www.youtube.com/watch?v=Q6bvgIBPqrc

MORE FROM THE AUTHORS
You can read more from Frank Thomas and Valerie Melvin by visiting *www.franklygolf.com.*
Titles available include:
 Just Hit It: Our Equipment and Our Game
 Dear Frank: Answers to 100 of Your Golf Equipment Questions
 From Sticks and Stones: The Evolution of Golf Equipment Rules